B&T 19.50

The Sympathetic Response

The Sympathetic Response

George Eliot's Fictional Rhetoric

Mary Ellen Doyle, S.C.N.

Rutherford • Madison • Teaneck
Fairleigh Dickinson University Press

London and Toronto: Associated University Presses

© 1981 by Associated University Presses, Inc.

Associated University Presses, Inc.
4 Cornwall Drive
East Brunswick, New Jersey   08816

Associated University Presses Ltd.
69 Fleet Street
London EC4Y 1EU, England

Associated University Presses
Toronto, Ontario, Canada M5E 1A7

Library of Congress Cataloging in Publication Data

Doyle, Mary Ellen, 1932–
     The sympathetic response.

     Bibliography: p.
     Includes index.
     1. Eliot, George, pseud., i.e. Marian Evans, after-
wards Cross, 1819–1880––Technique. I. Title.
PR4691.D6   823′.8   80–65908
ISBN 0–8386–3065–0

Printed in the United States of America

Contents

to
Mary Doyle Springer and *Bernard J. Paris*
in gratitude

Acknowledgments

The most refreshingly honest comment from an author completing a book was made, I think, not by George Eliot, but by Mark Twain's blunt little ''river rat'': ''so there ain't nothing more to write about, and I am rotten glad of it, because if I'd 'a' knowed what a trouble it was to make a book I wouldn't 'a' tackled it, and ain't a'going to no more'' (''Chapter the Last'' of *Huckleberry Finn*).

This author, while admitting to those sentiments at moments, is compelled to write one more thing, which Huck omitted: that I, at least, could not have tackled a book, written and totally rewritten it, through many years and other occupations, through interruptions, setbacks, delays, and even a postal loss of the whole manuscript, had not many other people believed in its worth as doggedly and perversely as I myself did. These people—family, community, friends—demonstrated that belief by many kinds of psychological and material assistance; they brought me through the ''trouble it was''; they may even cause me to tackle a book again.

Among these many people, too numerous to mention by name, I must acknowledge with particular gratitude:

—first and always, the Sisters of Charity of Nazareth, the congregation and the many individuals in various positions, who gave me a start on literary studies and on this book, who continue to give personal and financial support, who did the typing and assisted in the editing;

—my teachers and friends at the University of Notre Dame, especially Professor Joseph Duffy, who roused my interest in George Eliot and directed my first study and writing about her;

—other friends, members of my family, and colleagues at Spalding College, Louisville, Kentucky, and at Nazareth Academy, Wakefield, Massachusetts, who continually encouraged, who took other jobs away so that I could write, and took me away, when necessary, so that I would rest from writing.

To the administration of Spalding College I am especially grateful for a sabbatical leave and a faculty grant that enabled me to complete the final draft.

I also thank the Widener Library at Harvard University for library privileges and numerous staff courtesies.

Two people above all others have contributed to this book:

My sister, Mary Doyle Springer, the first and better critic of literature, gave me all the support due from our family affection and literary friendship, but never let either interfere with her penetrating and honest critique of the work in progress. From the earliest drafts, she offered invaluable questions, suggestions, and insight; at one crucial stage she and her husband, Norman, gave me their sunny California home for a month of solitary writing. And at no stage would she let me quit.

To Professor Bernard J. Paris of Michigan State University I owe a debt not easily expressed. As a perfect stranger—and a perfect scholar—he took an interest in my work and sustained both the interest and the work through several years and revisions. Draft by draft, he read the manuscript; in margins, letters, phone calls, and a personal conference at his home, he discussed, criticized, corrected and approved, stimulated new ideas, approaches, and research. He let nothing go by, and, consequently, there is no part of the book that has not benefited from his attention. He has made me believe that the ''community of scholars'' is not a myth. And he has made himself (and his wife, Shirley) no longer a stranger but a friend.

These two people have given the book an unparalleled dedication. The book, therefore, is dedicated to them.

Introduction: The Rhetorical Approach

> The only effect I ardently long to produce by my writings, is that those who read them should be better able to *imagine* and to *feel* the pains and the joys of those who differ from themselves in everything but the broad fact of being struggling erring human creatures.[1]

In this characteristic statement, George Eliot clearly announces that her central aim as a writer is rhetorical. She wishes to influence the intellectual and emotional attitudes of real readers toward other real people in the real world outside her books. She proposes to do this by rousing those readers' imaginative sympathy for fictional people inside her books. Thus her method also is rhetorical; her fictional materials must be managed so as to produce the desired effects of understanding and sympathy. Her novels therefore invite rhetorical analysis as an effective way to grasp her art. The purpose of this book is to offer such an analysis.[2]

But rhetorical effect was not George Eliot's only goal. She also wished to make integrated works of art. Many of her letters, essays, and reviews assert her conviction, which she tried hard to follow, that fictions should be organic wholes, to which all parts should be necessary contributions. She refused to shorten *Middlemarch*, believing that it contained "nothing irrelevant to my design" (*GEL*, 5: 168), and she objected to a book of extracts from her works because her readers should be "moved towards the ends I seek by my works as wholes" (*GEL*, 5: 458).

Two such goals engender a literary problem. A rhetorical aim that lies outside the fiction can be in conflict with the aim of making an integrated artifact. To real people one can presumably give almost unlimited imaginative concern, but the degree of interest and sympathy accorded a fictional character must be limited by his importance in the whole novel. The artist, then, must seek to create within the novel a rhetoric proper to its achievement of organic unity, and the critic who undertakes a rhetorical analysis must harmonize that approach with formal analysis.[3] This harmonious critical approach can be sought in terms of the ''expectations'' aroused and satisfied in a novel.

To begin with, the very fact that a work is a novel generates the expectation of a structured tale, a story presenting characters in relationships and actions. The actions, we expect, will be plotted to achieve an outcome that will have some definite emotional direction and effect. We also expect that the novel will offer some theme or meaning relative to human experience, which meaning will emerge from the characterizations and the achieved plot. While all novels must meet this very general structural expectation, particular novels have variations in their patterns due chiefly to the kind of interest or emotional effect each novel is striving for. We describe a specific novel partly by identifying that effect—usually as comic, serious, or tragic; and we expect all other elements to contribute to its ultimate achievement. As formal theorists have often asserted, the emotional intention of a fiction (its effect, *dynamis*, power) is demonstrably a controlling factor in its formal wholeness.[4]

The initial expectation that a novel will be a patterned whole generates the correlative expectation that the parts will exhibit aesthetic proportion. We expect that the actions will be sufficient in their number and development to elucidate the characters and credibly bring about the denouement. The characters, we assume, will be developed in proportion to their function. We expect our interest in them to be proportionate to their importance; we expect to be duly aroused but not carried away, and ultimately to be satisfied by the denouement that concludes their fictional lives.

Signals given early in the novel create our initial expectations about what kind of pattern we shall have—comic, serious, tragic—and what proportioning of characters, actions, and interest will be appropriate. But it is not at all evident how the final patterning will be achieved. Our curiosity, fear, hope, and spirit of prophecy are repeatedly activitated as one thing leads to another, as one action or character invites a response, suggests a meaning, or generates an expectation.[5] Therefore, in every novel we expect and accept a "holding pattern" in the further expectation that the completed pattern will have coherence and will reconcile the various interests and emotions aroused.

In view of these various expectations, we may say that the ultimate unity of a novel lies both in its formal pattern and in its preparation of the audience's experience of that pattern. The parts, as we read them, generate expectations that we demand to have fulfilled in the whole. Various rhetorical techniques put (or should put) all these parts together into a satisfying whole; our sense of the intended whole (which may not be actually achieved) then becomes the norm by which we judge the rhetorical effectiveness of the parts. Rhetoric helps to create form; form is used to judge the rhetoric. Some of the artistic problems in George Eliot's novels—in *Middlemarch*, for a prime example—can be explained by the way early parts create a distinct notion of the intended whole, which is then violated by later parts.

At this point two elucidations seem desirable. Since all novels arouse "expectations" and some emotions in readers, it follows that all novels are, in some degree, rhetorical in their effects and methods, whether or not these are consciously intended or employed by the author. George Eliot's novels differ only in that rhetorical intent and methodology are manifested in a high degree and in that internal evidence is backed up by her explicit statements of desire to influence real readers' responses. All novels are rhetorical; Victorian novels are more rhetorical than most, and George Eliot's may be the most deliberately rhetorical of all. Hence hers especially invite and reward the rhetorical approach to analysis.

Next, it may be advisable to elucidate further the definition of *rhetoric* that underlies this book. The term has had almost as many definitions from ancient to modern times as has *plot*.[6] In its broadest sense, it means the entire management of audience response. In this management, the writer uses all the elements and techniques of fiction that modern critics analyze separately: character interaction, structure of events, viewpoint, language, et cetera. Rhetoric, like the child confronted with the basket of toys, "chooses everything"; and the critic of rhetoric is under much the same compulsion.

However, though rhetoric uses all the tools of fiction, it usually has a special purpose for their deployment, a special kind of audience response that it seeks to rouse. Like plot (if we can accept the categories of Crane[7]), rhetoric can choose one of three "synthesizing principles." It might be aimed chiefly at winning intellectual and emotional assent to the theme proposed. It might be aimed at rousing the reader's anger, pity, revulsion, or admiration in regard to a situation or set of related situations; this would be true, for instance, of novels (like many of Dickens's) that primarily attack social injustices. Or the rhetoric may be focused on the characters and their fates, to which their situations contribute more or less; this is certainly the mode of George Eliot's highly mimetic novels (*Silas Marner* will be discussed as an exception). We are disgusted by the situation of women in Victorian societies like St. Ogg's and Middlemarch, but only because we are first so vitally concerned about the two heroines crushed in those social presses.

According to the kind of audience response the novelist chiefly desires, one aspect or mode of rhetorical management may be central. Because George Eliot's primary aim was the sympathetic response of readers to characters, a key aspect of her rhetoric and a most useful focus for rhetorical analysis is the concept of "distance" as it has been developed in modern criticism.[8]

Distance refers to the precise degree of the reader's involvement with or detachment from a character. It can be intellectual (interest and understanding or the lack of them) or emotional (sympathy or aversion). If it is "right distance," it is established according to that character's role and purpose in the novel. For the critic, distance can be a password and a light leading into and through the almost limitless caverns of rhetoric. It is possible to examine other rhetorical effects and techniques by showing their effects upon distance.

This book will examine George Eliot's fictional rhetoric in five novels, with a focus on her increasing achievement of right distance according to the requirements of the formal whole. It will examine in each novel its internal norms for distance and the techniques by which George Eliot succeeds or fails in achieving it rightly. Examination of each novel will involve three basic questions: What is the formal whole of the novel—its central concern and consequent structural pattern? Given that whole, what kind and degree of interest or sympathy should we accord to the various characters?[9] And finally, how are the apprehension of the whole and the responses to the characters conditioned by various rhetorical techniques?

The Formal Whole as Norm for Distance

The shortest way to the whole of a fiction is the time-honored, instinctive question, ''What is it about?'' The answer will have some such frame as ''It is a story about . . . which means this.'' The description of the whole, that is, should identify the protagonist(s), the central issue and type of outcome, the basic kinds of characters and events that must develop that issue, and the thematic meaning. If the novel is a true whole, all the events and characters can be accounted for by their relation to the central issue, and the structural arrangements of the story will support that relationship. The theme will emerge consistently from the events by which the characters arrive at the resolution of the central issue. What-happens-to-whom will not seem to imply one meaning in one part of the novel and an altogether different meaning in another part. Theme will be integral to the whole form; we shall not be able to extract it like a plum from a pudding.[10]

Most very long novels, of course, are not perfect wholes; and George Eliot's are no exception. Every one of her novels has aroused critical debate about its unity. It is my opinion that all the novels to be discussed in this study, except *Daniel Deronda*, have identifiable central issues and coherent, describable patterns, but that all have significant deviations from their patterns and consequent rhetorical flaws. *Deronda* lacks a single organizing issue to unify it; the other novels have one, but different aspects of their rhetoric set up different sets of expectations, not all of which can be satisfied.

Here I simply acknowledge that the persuasiveness of my argument about each novel will rest on my reader's agreement with my description of the whole. That description will flow from a close reading, the closest I could make, of both the novel and criticism of it. If I found and could accept a general consensus on the what-it's-about and what-it-means, I could simply use that as a starting point for rhetorical analysis. But about some novels no consensus has ever been achieved, either about the subject of the whole (*Adam Bede*, *Felix Holt*) or about the fitness and meaning of a major part (Maggie's and Dorothea's denouements). The lack of consensus on these matters after decades of critical debate is a clear sign of some serious flaw in the novels. As any critic must in a debate, I take my stand and try to explain what I see to be awry. And whatever else the flaw may be—in structure, narrative diction or tone, et cetera—it is sure to be also a flaw in the rhetoric.

Once described, the whole offers criteria for the distancing of characters. These norms follow from the function of rhetoric, which is to reinforce the pattern of the novel by controlling both the kind and amount of sympathy accorded to the characters. "Kind" involves such interests as practical concern for a character's welfare or sympathy for his personal traits. These are not really the same as a high interest in his individuality, which is a matter of degree or amount. In a protagonist we are apt to take all kinds of interest in a high degree, but a character like Bulstrode can fascinate us without our minding much what will happen to him or liking his moral qualities. Both the kind and amount of sympathy must be rhetorically managed to meet the requirements of form. As the formal whole is described by its plot and theme, so the criteria for distance may be explicated by the characters' roles in the plot and their relation to the theme.

First of all, our emotional concern for a character's happiness must be balanced with our aesthetic and intellectual response to his role in the novel's plot, be that comic, serious, or tragic.[11] In the case of a comic plot, balance is rather easily achieved; what must happen according to form is what we want to happen anyway. Not so in most serious and in all tragic plots; the practical outcome for the protagonist could be or certainly will be disastrous, and our desire for his well-being is in conflict with our aesthetic wish to see the pattern completed. So the formal pattern must be made to harmonize with the emotional or rhetorical effects. Once a serious or tragic pattern is set, it must be completed, even at the expense of a likable character's happiness or success; and the rhetoric must enable the reader to take aesthetic pleasure in the outcome despite his practical wishes and sympathies. From a tragic protagonist the reader must be at a distance sufficient to endure his destruction, and from a serious protagonist sufficient to observe his trials with some equanimity and even be glad of them.

George Eliot wrote no strictly comic novels; her happy-ending novels are fundamentally serious. Despite the Mesdames Poyser, Bede, and Holt, Adam Bede's and Felix Holt's struggles for personal fulfillment and marital joy are not presented as matter for humorous or satiric treatment. And *The Mill on the Floss* and *Middlemarch* have essentially tragic patterns. All Eliot's main characters suffer, and some are literally or figuratively destroyed. In her best work, aesthetic interest in pattern and practical interest in a character's happiness are either in harmony or in a constructive tension that contributes to our emotional experience and comprehension and that is finally resolved if we can accept the pattern and theme of the novel as a whole. Her failures in rhetoric often result from unresolved tension between these two kinds of interest, from fuzziness or incongruity in the pattern itself, or from a sacrifice of pattern to obtain a strong practical interest. These three errors will at least describe the probably insoluble Ladislaw controversy.

As formal pattern necessitates a balance of aesthetic and practical concerns, so it also dictates that the amount of interest and sympathy generated for any character should be limited by his relative importance in the whole novel. Not even the most engaging character is entitled to a life independent of his function in the total context. It is not necessarily good that we know all about a given character or feel intensely with him, nor can deeply moving events depicted in powerful scenes always be praised without qualification. They may cause the character to overpower other characters whose fate is meant to be more intimately related to the central issue or more permanently consequential in the novel. Because of George Eliot's overdevelopment of Hetty Sorrel, many a critic has taken her fate as the central issue of *Adam Bede* and has objected to the final development of Dinah Morris in Book 6. These imbalances are most apt to occur when George Eliot seems not fully certain herself what the novel's central issue is, or, if certain, not in control of the pattern needed to elucidate that issue. Impartial analysis of *The Mill on the Floss*, for instance, must note the flaws in its focus and organization and the resultant imbalance in the distancing of all four major characters.

Problems with distancing according to a character's role in the plot are indigenous to the representation of highly mimetic characters such as George Eliot's. The more realistic they become, the more they tend to individuality and the more they interest our minds and engage our emotions. Then the more we care for them as individuals, the less we care if they break limits and damage either the house of fiction or the less interesting people in it. In the case of George Eliot's people, the danger is compounded because she aimed to achieve just such an engaged reaction, and she herself was sometimes beguiled by character to the neglect of form. She recognized that she had been so beguiled in writing *The Mill on the Floss* (GEL, 3: 317), though possibly she never realized how severe was the ultimate damage to both its form and its rhetoric.

Another set of criteria for distance is established by a character's relation to the theme of the whole novel, its controlling vision of meaning and value in the lives depicted. *Meaning* and *value* imply standards of intellectual and moral worth, of general significance or irrelevancy, wisdom or folly in human life and conduct. In a formally whole novel, the standards implied should add up to a unified theme, and the characters should be rhetorically placed at a distance that accords with that theme.

At this point, a *caveat* may be appropriate. In the matter of distancing according to theme, if anywhere, rhetorical art and mature reading are urgently needed, because here, if anywhere, both artist and reader may disengage from the formal whole and impose personal likes and dislikes, approval and disapproval, sympathies and antipathies, all unrelated to form. This is not to insist that an actual reader can—or even should—put his personal criteria in total abeyance.[12] Inevitably, his own sense of the character's merits, his own beliefs and values will be standards by which he distances himself from both character and implied author. Nevertheless, the mature reader must try to enter the author's frame of reference, to perceive the standards implied within the novel, and to let these be his bases for appropriate response and final aesthetic judgment.

To gain this kind of response from the reader, the author must first guarantee that the standards offered are consistent, so that a sense of thematic closure is achieved, so that one coherent meaning does emerge from the many meanings that inhere in the many characters and actions. According to that one meaning which is everywhere implied, we should be able to respond consistently as we read. This does not deny that shifting reactions to a character are a valid part of both internal rhetoric and reader response; such shifts are part of the ''holding pattern'' we expect as the ultimate meaning emerges. But our teeth should not be constantly jarred by radical shifts.

Then the author must consistently apply the standards to the characters so that the working out of their lives coheres with the central meaning. No character should escape from what the whole novel seems to be saying. Nor should one set of standards apply to a given character in one part of the novel and a sharply different and incompatible set apply in another. The meaning of a character's life direction should not be turned about in the middle of a novel. What means tragic diminution in one part cannot, without *very* convincing rhetoric, be made to mean glorious fulfillment in another part. The attempt to switch meanings violates previously created expectations, confuses the distance of reader from character, and calls forth either contradictory or ambiguous responses. In this kind of rhetorical confusion we can locate most of the problems with Maggie Tulliver and with Dorothea Brooke's second love and marriage.

As highly mimetic characters tend to break their limits on the degree of interest dictated by their role in the central issue, so do they break limits on the kind of distance dictated by theme. In Scholes and Kellogg's terms,[13] such mimetic characters are "representational"; they are realistically portrayed in much detail, and they invite psychological and sociological analysis. However, even the most representational characters are also "illustrative" in some measure; what they say and do means something, something usually expressed in ethical or metaphysical terms. If the novel is an integrated whole, the representational and illustrative roles will cohere. And the kind of distance called for by the rhetoric at any point (intellectual agreement, moral antipathy, amused detachment, tragic pity, etc.) will be appropriate both to what is actually going on (representation) and to what it means (illustration). But it is evident that what characters say and do, especially when represented in plentiful and realistic detail, can violate what they are supposed to mean. And if war obtains either between two illustrative functions (Will as great lover, bravely chosen, v. Will as second-rate but best available choice) or between illustrative and mimetic (what Maggie and Dorothea are supposed to illustrate thematically and what

the represented facts show about them), then the unity of
rhetorical effect is destroyed in the clash. The reader will, as a
rule, be compelled to respond most strongly to the force of powerful representation and will approve or disapprove, feel tragedy or
mere pathos, get involved or stay detached, according to what
words and actions show the character to be, not according to what
the other rhetorical devices say he/she is supposed to mean.

Of course, represented character and thematic meaning may
not be simply *different*. It may also be true that the theme is partially accurate to the characters and is even internally coherent
and consistently applied, but is still inadequate for the range and
complexity of the characters depicted. In that case, the artist's
power to interpret all he sees is deficient, from lack of penetration,
wisdom, or whatever. Perhaps this deficiency does not matter,
since novelists need not be philosophers or pastors; and we can
certainly learn much for our own growth in wisdom by analyzing
the deficiency.[14] For rhetorical analysis, however, the question is
still one of formal wholeness and unity. If the interpretation in
any part of the novel or the whole does not fit the represented
facts, so that we cannot believe the meaning assigned, then we
cannot respond to the rhetorical signals.

And because the signals elicit responses, which create our
sense of the whole, by which we judge the technical signals, we
are back on the circle of form-rhetoric, a circle that either is rup-
tured and leaves us to admire significant and lovely fragments, or
is whole and carries us around from one pleasure to another,
always somehow moved by all its parts simultaneously. George
Eliot's novels, we must say, are generally circles with a broken
arc, nearly enough whole to show the intended form and meaning, powerful enough rhetorically to move us deeply by what they
show.

Techniques for Distancing

When we have described the formal pattern of a novel and
determined the proper distance for any character, we can then

proceed to a technical analysis to see if and how that distance has actually been achieved. Of all the rhetorical techniques, narrative voice and point-of-view have received the most attention, thanks to Wayne Booth, but as he himself recognized,[15] a complete rhetoric of fiction would have to include consideration of how character, events, structure, and language affect reader response. Narrative voice, however, is a good place to begin discussion of technique, because the distances between character, author, and reader are established through the narrator. Between each possible pair, as it were, stands the narrator as a possible bond or disruptive influence, according to his own relation to each.

The sympathetic bond George Eliot desired her readers to have with her characters depends on the distance between the narrator and the character. In a thousand ways the story-telling personality projects his attitudes toward the fictional people and thus influences the attitudes of the reader.[16] Since George Eliot used omniscient narration in the expansive Victorian manner, her reader may expect both elaborate representations and frank appraisals of character. The question of discrepancy between representation and interpretation, already discussed, arises and is most felt in this narrator-character relationship. We can say that we have a right to expect of a narrator enough wisdom to comprehend his facts and to apply consistently his own standards for judgment and sympathy. By these standards, George Eliot's narrators seem generally reliable interpreters. They understand the characters intimately, and they like or dislike them according to their deserts. But there are several very troublesome exceptions. At times, George Eliot's narrators seem to have emotional reactions unwarranted by the facts of the characters' behavior. These exceptions, especially in the cases of Maggie Tulliver and Dorothea Brooke, have led critics into endless discussions of the distance—or lack of it—between the characters and George Eliot.

Any problem of distance between author and character involves a problem of distance between author and narrator. Even in the omniscient mode there is never a complete identity between a narrator and an author. The narrator is not just a pose that the author adopts, though George Eliot did, in her early work, attempt such poses as that of the "real" masculine narrator who discussed events with his friend Adam Bede.[17] For rhetorical purposes, the narrator should be a means by which the author may attain and maintain the objectivity essential to a correct placement of the characters. If the author fails in this, the reader is jarred and emotionally disoriented by a sudden discrepancy between the speaking storyteller and the authorial mind implied in and governing the book.[18] The narrator, for instance, may be urging sympthetic understanding, while a few ill-chosen words cause the author to show through as deficient in this very quality. Some of the descriptions of Hetty Sorrel's vain musings will serve as examples of this defect.

Or the narrator may be showing so uneven a rhetorical style, so great a tension between concurrent impulses to laugh at a character's folly and to sympathize with his (mostly *her*) grandeur and pain, that the author's lack of objectivity is plainly seen. Fortunately for her use of the omniscient mode, George Eliot did not fail frequently in this author-narrator relation; but unfortunately, her worst failures were with protagonists, especially her two chief heroines.

If the narrator is to maneuver the distance between reader and character and to place the author in relation to both, it follows that the narrator himself must have a third relation, that to the reader. No author can envision all actual readers; but he can know the mentality he would like his readers to have. The relation that he constructs through his narrator, therefore, is not with the real person who peruses his novel, but with the "mock-reader," a fictively projected person of particular intellectual and moral traits who he implies is reading and reacting to the book.[19] Most readers, especially if educated, are willing to modify and universalize their daily selves to engage in a literary experience, but not to the extent of abrogating all personal traits, values, and judgments or of conforming to minds totally antithetic. If the mock-reader, for instance, is clearly expected to take an attitude of condescension that the real reader feels is arrogant, the latter will simply distance himself from the narrator and his directions. (Obviously, the necessity of making interpretation fit the facts reenters here.) The finesse of distancing, therefore, is largely a matter of the narrator's projecting a mock-reader with whom any intelligent, decent, and fair-minded actual reader can identify. For if we can accept his attitudes toward our imagined selves, we are likely to make the suggested responses to the characters.

Though the three relationships of the narrator just described generate the most obvious kind of rhetorical control, the characters and events of a novel also exert rhetorical force. The rhetoric of character is more than the mimetic representation that makes a character live for us. It encompasses all the ways in which characters are given their rightful degrees of importance in the novel and are placed against each other so that each affects the responses the reader gives to all.

To a large degree, our interest in a character and sense of his importance are controlled by the extent to which he is developed. The character who appears often, is described in considerable detail, speaks volubly, and is active in emotionally charged scenes will inevitably rouse a considerable degree either of interest and sympathy or of aversion. If all the feeling he arouses is not warranted by his role in the novel, then such an elaborate depiction is excessive. By it, the character unquestionably is made an absorbing and memorable figure and a source of great pleasure to the reader. But he may cause other characters to be underrepresented and thus denied the greater degree of interest and importance due to them. It just may be that we see too much of Mrs. Poyser, the Dodsons, and the schoolboy Tom Tulliver, and too little of Dinah Morris, Felix Holt, and the adult Tom.

The placement of characters in relation to each other also has strong rhetorical effect. The juxtaposition of Hetty Sorrel and Dinah Morris responding to Thias Bede's death constitutes a rhetoric that initially fixes our basic respect for Dinah and alienation from Hetty and prepares all our future responses to both. The contrast of Dorothea and Celia Brooke reacting to Casaubon is more subtle, in that comparisons invoke both sympathy with and satiric laughter at all three. We must, of course, see enough of any characters who affect our distance from other characters. Persons influencing each other significantly must either be brought together fairly often or be convincingly related through a third party. Part of the problem in winning the reader's assent to the marriage of Adam Bede and Dinah Morris lies in their long separation and the weakness of Seth Bede as a link.

Interrelationships of characters are especially relevant to a discussion of distance in George Eliot's novels because she uses such a number and variety of fictional persons and consistently sets up occasions for their interaction that raise our hopes and fears for them. Interaction implies events; these also function rhetorically.

The rhetoric of events is quite potent and obvious in its effects. Clearly, a reader's imaginative engagement in a novel's episodes will cause strong and varied emotional responses. We like or dislike, pity or blame characters largely by what they do. Technically, an artist manipulates episodes so as to get the desired responses, either from the event in itself or from the way one event impinges on another.

In itself, an event affects us rhetorically both by its content and its manner of presentation. The action will be, by its nature, delightful or amusing, frightening, appalling, or repulsive; so also will be the characters who act. A reader will ordinarily become most involved in a scene that is long, detailed, and emotionally charged; by contrast, an event will be less engaging if it is narratively summarized, is dramatized but foreshortened, or is emotionally low-keyed or undercut by humor or satire. Yet apparently diverse combinations of these modes of presentation can create powerful rhetorical effects. The scenes between Lydgate and Rosamond after their marriage, for instance, represent their words, movements, and gestures in detail; but the emotional manner is low pitched and intensely, ominously quiet. Neither partner rants or dramatizes the event. The result for the reader is an intense emotional awareness of Rosamond's mannered inflexibility and Lydgate's ironic helplessness, also of the intense disappointment in false and unworthy dreams that both are suffering. Rosamond is vastly distanced, and Lydgate becomes immensely pitiable; but neither is wholly exonerated or condemned, as might have been true had their contest been presented as a brawl.

To be rhetorically effective, events must be of a kind and quantity sufficient to explain and render credible the characters involved, especially if those events are preparation for others even more important. It is not easy to credit Maggie Tulliver's late assertion that Tom was once ''good to her,'' since almost no events have demonstrated such goodness. And the dramatized marital encounters of Grandcourt and Gwendolen are perfect in kind but perhaps not numerous enough to generate all the comprehension and sympathy we need to lessen our previous alienation from Gwendolen and to prepare our understanding of her actions and feelings at Grandcourt's drowning. Obviously, events must be consistent with the moral and intellectual qualities of the characters who act, or their inconsistency must be explainable. The kindly Poysers' rejection of their imprisoned niece is a strong factor in our growing sympathy for her, but it would be merely a trick generating sentimentality and we would refuse to respond were it not for previous signs of their fixation in a code and for the narrator's convincing explanation of their act.

Events also impinge on each other rhetorically by their placement in the novel; this is a matter of structure. Modern criticism has taken notice of structural devices used to achieve special rhetorical effects.[20] These devices include the sequential arrangement of chapters, uses of initial and terminal positions for emphasis, juxtapositons and special placements of any sort, inversions of chronology, large jumps or gaps in time reference, direct or implied repetitions and parallels. Many of these structural devices work together; juxtaposition, for instance, can create awareness of a parallel that otherwise might go unobserved. George Eliot was never to use such extreme complications of sequence or style as we are accustomed to in this century, but she does increasingly employ sophistication of structure so that one person or event is constantly and strikingly affecting our response to another. *Middlemarch*, despite its several plots and subplots, its numerous characters and their analogous relationships, coheres and compels our vital interest largely through this careful rhetoric of structure.

The language of narration and dialogue has special relevance to control over distance. Characters are represented in words, the narrator's or their own. And words make characters vivid, impressive, sympathetic or antipathetic, according as those words are abstract or concrete, general or particular, formal, informal or colloquial, positive or negative in connotation, merely descriptive or essentially evaluative. Exactly what is a ''thrilling'' voice, and who is, or is supposed to be, thrilled? Exactly what is said about Dorothea Brooke by incessantly calling her ''ardent''? Such words imply attitudes, those of characters to each other and of the narrator and implied author to the characters and mock-reader; hence the words and implied attitudes generate a reaction in the reader toward all those persons. Quite evidently a single word or a metaphor can specify a narrator's attitude to a character and irrevocably condition—or confuse—that of a reader. An exclamation, a series of adjectives, can make a knowing, just, and compassionate narrator seem suddenly vindictive, or can wreck the favorable attitude he wants us to adopt. A comparison of the narrative diction employed on Hetty Sorrel and Rosamond Vincy, both basically antipathetic women, shows how much George Eliot could and did learn about word choice. Similarly, a character whose speeches are too many or too few, stilted, or inconsistent can seem simply unknowable in any degree requisite for sympathy. If Dinah Morris and Felix Holt could change their speech patterns, they and their love experiences would be far more credible. And no one, in or outside of *Middlemarch*, except Dorothea and *perhaps* the narrator, seems to comprehend or care much for Ladislaw, victim of both the narrator's description and his own language.

All the techniques of rhetoric just discussed can, of course, affect readers without their realizing it. The level of realization depends on the perceptiveness and sensitivity of actual readers, of whom a critic can speak for only one—himself. Furthermore, no one experiences all techniques simultaneously in the same degree, especially not on the first reading.[21] The holding pattern discussed earlier operates to restrain, even deliberately confuse, our responses until the whole is complete and we can make our final assessment of each character and then analyze what caused it. In the first reading of a modern novel, our responses may be wholly conditioned by dislocations of time sequence, delayed or inaccurate disclosures, or narration through disturbed minds; second and subsequent readings are totally different experiences. A first reading of a George Eliot novel is never so puzzling as that, but uncertainty and initial reactions to personalities may well overpower our consciousness of her technical nuances. Only later may we realize how skillfully she has constructed a network of narrative techniques to control our sympathetic responses.

A critic of fictional rhetoric, then, has to construct his own mock-reader, one willing to explore George Eliot's works as often as necessary to discover what is demonstrably there, on whichever reading he finds it. And the critic can elucidate only what techniques he himself has found to be operative and can evaluate how well they have worked only by his own perception of the completed whole. For authorial skills and achievements he has failed to observe or has misunderstood, he is, of course, accountable to other critics.

In the nineteenth century, most novelists at least began their writing with characters in fairly predictable relations and with an omniscient narrator commenting freely upon them and genially imposing explicit guidance on a ''dear Reader,'' who probably responded just as desired. The events were told in simple chronological sequence and straightforward language. George Eliot's beginnings were hardly exceptional. But as her characters and their problems became more subtle and her narrator more sophisticated, so did her structural and linguistic techniques for controlling our responses to them. By the time of *Middlemarch*, she had reached a skill in devising fictional rhetoric that has placed and kept her in the front rank of novelists of that or any other century.

This study will offer an analysis and evaluation of *Adam Bede*, *The Mill on the Floss, Felix Holt the Radical, Middlemarch*, and *Daniel Deronda* in terms of the norms and techniques discussed in this introduction. These novels were selected for their importance in the George Eliot canon, their continuing popularity among her readers, their similarities and significant differences, and, above all, their susceptibility to this type of analysis. George Eliot's other fictions are omitted chiefly to avoid repetitiveness and excess length in this book, but they are briefly discussed in their chronological sequence in order to note their significant differences from the other novels and their place in George Eliot's development.

Though complicated by the abundance of her means, a rhetorical analysis of George Eliot's work illuminates both the separate novels and the path of her artistic development. She knew what she wanted to do and, in years of practicing her art, learned ever better how to do it. By following the ''how'' to her peak of achievement, we may find ourselves more deeply responsive to what we see, and profoundly enriched by ''that increase in sympathy and understanding, that moral enlargement which is the end to which all George Eliot's aesthetic means are directed.''[22]

Notes

1. George Eliot to Charles Bray, 5 July 1859, *The George Eliot Letters*, ed. Gordon S. Haight, 7 vols. (New Haven, Conn.: Yale University Press, 1954-55), 3:111. Hereafter cited as *GEL*.

2. For the initial interest and technical awareness that led to this book, I acknowledge gratefully Wayne Booth's *The Rhetoric of Fiction* (Chicago: University of Chicago Press, 1961). In a sense, I attempt in this book to develop his observations, partly in theory but chiefly by practical application to specific novels. My later awareness of ficitional rhetoric has been assisted by the series ''Towards a Poetics of Fiction'' in *Novel: A Forum on Fiction* 1 and 2 (1967-69).

3. Quite evidently, the many other approaches to fictional analysis developed in the last thirty years—mimetic, linguistic, psychological, thematic, historical-cultural, biographical—can all be brought to bear in a rhetorical analysis, and all have contributed in some measure to my understanding of George Eliot's rhetoric. My indebtedness to the theorists of these approaches will be seen in my bibliography. I employ their methods, but only incidentally, in part because limitations must be selected for a finite study, in chief

part because they do not offer distinct criteria for rhetoric in the same degree offered (in my opinion) by the formal approach. Mimesis, for instance, was highly important to George Eliot's rhetorical intention since the people in her books would have to approximate those in the real world. But though she herself believed that realistic portrayal of ordinary lives was the best, even the only way to produce moral sympathy in readers, realism remains a technique for rhetorical achievement, not a criterion for evaluating it.

4. R. S. Crane, "The Concept of Plot and the Plot of 'Tom Jones,' " in *Critics and Criticism*, ed. R. S. Crane (Chicago: University of Chicago Press, Phoenix Books, 1957), pp. 66-69; Crane, *The Language of Criticism and the Structure of Poetry* (Toronto: University of Toronto Press, 1953); Norman Friedman, "Forms of the Plot," in *The Theory of the Novel*, ed. Philip Stevick (New York: The Free Press, 1967), pp. 145-66; Sheldon Sacks, *Fiction and the Shape of Belief* (Berkeley: University of California Press, 1964), chap. 1; Mary D. Springer, *Forms of the Modern Novella* (Chicago: University of Chicago Press, 1975), chap. 1. My very general description of what we expect in a novel will, I hope, encompass all the specific kinds described by these formal theorists, to whom I am most indebted, on whose observations I dare attempt to build.

5. Wolfgang Iser, *The Implied Reader: Patterns of Communication in Prose Fiction from Bunyan to Beckett* (Baltimore, Md.: The Johns Hopkins University Press, 1974), pp. 279-88, discusses these effects with a focus on the psychology of the reader rather than on the patterning of the whole novel itself.

6. Our modern sense of the term as applied to fictional rhetoric is most dependent, I believe, on Booth. A review of meanings and an explication of the term is also offered by David Lodge, *Language of Fiction: Essays in Criticism and Verbal Analysis of the English Novel* (London: Routledge and Kegan Paul, 1966), p. 147.

7. Crane, "Concept of Plot," pp. 66-67.

8. Booth, especially chaps. 5, 6, 9; Edward Bullough, " 'Psychical Distance' as a Factor in Art and an Aesthetic Principle," in *The Problems of Aesthetics*, eds. Eliseo Vivas and Murray Krieger (New York: Holt, Rinehart and Winston, 1953), pp. 396-405; David Daiches, *A Study of Literature for Readers and Critics* (Ithaca, N.Y.: Cornell University Press, 1948), pp. 63-65; Richard Eastman, *A Guide to the Novel* (San Francisco, Calif.: Chandler Publications, 1965), p. 53.

9. Because the term *sympathy* will be used very often in this book, it too should be clarified. As used here it can designate three qualities: simple pity, a sense of mental or moral compatibility, and that deep intellectual and imaginative union which makes the reader thoroughly comprehend what it would be like to be a given character. Any or all three forms of sympathy can be elicited by one character (Lydgate, for a prime example); all three must, therefore, enter into a discussion of the rhetoric by which response to characters is controlled. The context of the discussion will, I hope, make clear which meaning pertains.

10. For a full discussion of the relation of form and meaning, cf. Norman Friedman, *Form and Meaning in Fiction* (Athens: University of Georgia Press, 1975), chap. 10.

11. The various and conflicting kinds of interest in fiction are discussed by Booth, pp. 125-36.

12. Booth, pp. 137-44, defends the role of belief in the personal experience of reading and evaluating. A partial and effective dissent from Booth is offered by Bernard J. Paris, *A Psychological Approach to Fiction* (Bloomington: Indiana University Press, 1974), pp. 16-20.

13. Robert Scholes and Robert Kellogg, *The Nature of Narrative* (New York: Oxford University Press, 1966), pp. 83-91.

14. Paris, *A Psychological Approach to Fiction*, chap. 1, elucidates helpfully the distinction between representation and interpretation of character. I differ only in degree from his assessment of the importance of accurate interpretation. A discrepancy between representation and interpretation both diminishes the thematic significance of the novel and causes aesthetic incoherence, flaws that I consider more serious than does Paris, less redeemable by brilliant realistic representation of a human psyche.

15. Booth, *"The Rhetoric of Fiction* and the Poetics of Fictions,'' *Novel: A Forum on Fiction* 1 (1968): pp. 105-17.

16. Cf. Paul Goodman, *The Structure of Literature* (Chicago: University of Chicago Press, 1954), pp. 75-77, 117-19, 153-59; Kathleen Tillotson, *The Tale and the Teller* (London: Rupert Hart-Davis, 1959), passim.

17. A writer on George Eliot's technique must inevitably fuss with the question of the narrator's sex and the resulting choice of personal pronouns. The ''real'' and seemingly masculine narrator of *Adam Bede* is not maintained even throughout that novel, and in all the other novels, George Eliot projects a narrative persona that is obviously close to herself, a woman speaking from feminine experience and perspective. To solve the pronoun dilemma, therefore, I have chosen to use masculine pronouns in the theoretical Introduction and in the chapter on *Adam Bede* and feminine pronouns in all other chapters.

18. Cf. Bullough, pp. 400-402; Walter J. Slatoff, *With Respect to Readers* (Ithaca, N.Y.: Cornell University Press, 1970), p. 111.

19. Walker Gibson, ''Authors, Speakers, Readers and Mock-Readers,'' *College English* 11 (1950): pp. 265-69; cf. also Slatoff, pp. 54-56, 64-66, and Iser, Introduction and chap. 11. Iser's ''implied reader'' is essentially a real reader outside the novel whose reading processes Iser analyzes. This book's approach requires analysis of the reader created or implied inside the novel. To maintain the distinction clearly, I have retained the term *mock-reader*, originally Gibson's.

20. In addition to the formalist critics already cited, cf. Malcolm Bradbury, ''Towards a Poetics of Fiction: 1) An Approach through Structure,'' *Novel: A Forum on Fiction* 1 (1967): 45-52; Eastman, passim; Goodman, pp. 160-61; René Wellek and Austin Warren, *Theory of Literature* (New York: Harcourt, Brace and Company, 1942), pp. 201-15.

21. Cf. Slatoff, pp. 19-20.

22. W. J. Harvey, *The Art of George Eliot* (New York: Oxford University Press, 1962), p. 148.

[2]

Adam Bede

> Mr. Elliot [*sic*] is good enough to tell us . . . that people are not so bad as is commonly supposed . . . . The novel before us is crowded with characters, but they are loveable. . . . The author finds good in them all and lets them off easy, not only with pardon, but . . . loaded with sympathy.[1]

This early review of *Adam Bede* is fairly typical of the kind of interest and feeling the novel roused in the Victorians—a warm, generalized, largely indiscriminate sympathy for all the characters. Modern critics have tended to assert their own and what they believe to be George Eliot's likes and dislikes of separate characters and to evaluate the novel in terms of the justice of those feelings. The primary question, though, must be whether the author has so arranged her crowd of characters as to give her canvas a focus, an informing, controlling central issue, and has aided her reader to recognize this focus and to load on or withhold sympathy from the characters according to their relation to this issue. My answer is Yes, but with major reservations.

The issue is the humanistic education of one man, Adam Bede, his attainment of love and happiness through the rectification of his harsh character by suffering and learning to sympathize with the suffering of others, even those who caused his pain.[2] Two events chiefly occasion Adam's education to full humanity: the drowning of his drunken father and the disgrace and loss of Hetty Sorrel because of Arthur Donnithorne's seduction.[3] In reacting to these events, Adam is influenced by the other characters, and he finally integrates within himself their best qualities and values. Consequently, all other events and all other characters must seize our attention and sympathy only as much as will serve to advance our understanding of, interest in, and feeling for the central action—Adam's evolution to compassionate and universal love.

In structuring her plot, George Eliot met this basic formal requirement. At least twice as much space and elaboration of character is devoted to Adam as to any other individual or group. The novel begins with Adam, his work and family sorrows, and with a strong view of Dinah well before the introduction of Hetty; it ends with all of Book 6 devoted to the love-fulfillment of Adam and Dinah. In the first eighteen chapters, all the characters react in some way to Thias Bede's death, suggesting the event's importance and revealing their own personalities and probable influence on Adam. Only four short chapters (about one-fifth of this section) are given exclusively to initiating the affair of Arthur and Hetty.

This affair, which has most often preempted the main interest, is conducted with almost constant reference to its effect on Adam. The lovers' actions are always linked to him by Hetty's mental contrasting of him and Arthur, and by the recurring stress on Adam's love for her and his trust in Arthur as friend and patron. The climax of the seduction is rendered through Adam's view, not as it is experienced by the lovers. During the search for Hetty and the trial, everything is focused on Adam's suffering and learning, his temptation to revenge and achievement of sympathy. We are allowed to see the convulsion of Arthur's return, but not to focus again at any length on Arthur and Hetty. Adam and the reader alike are refused any account of the last meeting of the pair in prison, and George Eliot wisely ignored Blackwood's hint to dramatize the meeting of Arthur and Adam mentioned in the Epilogue (*GEL*, 2: 499).

Yet despite George Eliot's basic control of her main events, *Adam Bede* offers various problems concerning the interest and sympathy due to its scenes and characters. Its rhetorical strengths and flaws are found mainly in the way each character is used to control reader response to the others, especially to Adam. All other techniques may be studied most readily in relation to this one. This chapter therefore will examine the novel through the functions of the characters, minor and then major.

Normative Minor Characters

The minor characters all function as some type of norm for our judgment of the principals, especially of Adam. They must therefore be sympathetic according as they themselves approximate the ideal he must reach, and they must be represented in the degree necessary to depict his progress. The reader thus has a rhetorical relation to the characters themselves and also to Adam through them. Of these normative minor characters, the chief are Bartle Massey, Lisbeth and Seth Bede, Mr. Irwine, and the Hall Farm people.

Bartle Massey's role is small but significant. He appreciates and trains Adam's intelligence, regards him with affection, but is perceptive and frank enough to warn him of danger in his pride and temper (1:367, chap. 21). Thus he reflects what the reader should feel about Adam in the first part of the novel. He also reflects in himself Adam's negative possibility, because some similar suffering over a woman has left him a solitary misogynist. But, like Adam, he has a tender core that responds to the sight of suffering. By his own softened responses in reporting the trial, he reflects and encourages Adam's conversion to mercy. Thus the reader shares both his pity for Adam and his approval of the change.

Lisbeth Bede is a touchstone by which Adam's progress in sympathy is tested. To judge Adam, however, the reader must be more knowing than she, hence the narrator at once sets Lisbeth up in the proper light. Lisbeth is not wise, or "she would have gone away quietly, and said nothing" to her angry son (1:57, chap. 4); the narrator, however, *is* wise and can explain that Adam is justly vexed at her wailing but that Lisbeth is, nevertheless, a "good creature" (1:60, chap. 4). Adam must learn patience with her and respect for her judgment if he is to realize his full capacity for love.

Lisbeth is the main witness to Adam's faults towards his father. By testifying to Thias's good qualities and better days, she displays those facts which, along with kinship, should keep Adam merciful, and the reader accepts her verdict: "Thee mun forgie thy feyther—thee munna be so bitter again' him" (1:58, chap. 4).

Lisbeth's accurate judgment, seen in relation to Thias and Adam and also in her comic "nattering" of Seth, is the crucial preparation for her role in the denouement. If we were not already convinced of her powers of perception, we could hardly accept the swiftness of that event. As it is, her witty persuasion and Adam's new love for her combine to make it credible that she could so rapidly awaken him to his love for Dinah.

Seth Bede functions to display Adam's finer qualities and to keep him likable in his harsh period. He should therefore be Adam's inferior but still admirable so that the reader may engage with him in his continually affectionate regard for his brother. In general, Seth is a functionally successful character; yet George Eliot, like his mother, may be a bit unfair to him in pointing the contrast.

The opening scene establishes Adam by using Seth as a foil. Though the descriptions and dialogue are rendered without comment, they clearly suggest that Seth, though gentle, lovable, and by no means stupid, is also a pushover, absent-minded, and in need of his brother to defend him. Adam, by contrast, is the tallest, strongest man in the shop, prominent alike in his features and in the fine quality of his work. Despite his recurrent severity and lecturing, the weight of judgment is in his favor; one may like the mild man, but one prefers to ally with the strong. This is well enough, but some details seem inconsistent and unfair to Seth, gratuitously arranged to diminish him in contrast to Adam. Why, for instance, describe Adam's tone of address to his dog as "the same gentle modulation of voice as when he spoke to Seth"

(1:13, chap. 1)? Why should a projected partnership between the brothers envision Adam's doing "all the 'nice' work, that required peculiar skill" (1:317, chap. 19)? Would Seth really resemble an imbecile child "full o' thoughts he could give no account of; they'd never come t' anything, but they made him happy" (2:301, chap. 50)? Pushing Seth back does not draw Adam any closer to us.

Seth is Adam's foil not only in personal traits but as Dinah's lover. We understand her love for Adam by the contrast of his virility with Seth's mildness. We believe in Adam's ability to love her so deeply because of early evidence of his capacity for tenderness and self-revelation, exercised specifically and almost exclusively toward Seth. In his conjunction with Seth, we feel warmly sympathetic to Adam as a loving man.

But that does not remove all our difficulty in seeing Adam's final happiness in love depend on Seth's disappointment.[4] However structurally appropriate a second triangle may be, Seth does not deserve to lose Dinah as Arthur deserves his pain over Hetty. We like him too well to relish his loss even if we can stretch our imaginations enough to believe in his facile resignation. And however interesting this complication may be, it is not really needed; for Dinah could have been placed in Adam's path through her connection to the Poysers, and she could have felt his contrast to her fellow Methodist without having to reject the latter as a lover.

Lisbeth and Seth release Adam's initial capacity for patient love; the man who chiefly sustains it and teaches him to develop it is Mr. Irwine. To perform this function, the rector must be himself a man of merciful love and a trustworthy judge of human character, and he must be so presented as to make him fully sympathetic to the reader. He is all this in our first views of him in Chapter 5. Narrative description and his own concrete acts and words to his mother and sisters, Arthur, and Joshua Rann show him to be a "mixture of bonhommie and distinction" (1:81, chap. 5), of intelligent good humor toward the ignorant and patient sensitivity toward the weak. Later facts are equally in his favor. He is able to give Arthur, even without his explicit confession, a clear analysis of his weakness and the precise moral advice he needs. He constantly displays genial affection and understanding toward all the Hayslope community; this prepares us to identify with his deep compassion toward all concerned in the crisis and with his judgments of them, especially of Adam and Arthur.

Since facts strongly support Irwine as a normative character, little narrative interpretation would seem to be needed. But in her own day, apparently, George Eliot felt that it was. In Chapter 5 and again in Chapter 17, the narrator launches into special pleas for Irwine, defending him first against "Mr Roe, the 'travelling preacher,' " "a critical neighbour," and "honourable members zealous for the Church" who condemn his doctrinal and pastoral laxity (1:98, chap. 5), and then against "one of my readers (1:265, chap. 17) who wants the facts improved by a prevaricating and arbitrary artist. The purpose of these discourses is to reeducate the reader to a new kind of novel, very unlike the typical ecclesiastical or romantic fictions of the era, and thus to win his trust in the moral judgment of a seemingly imperfect cleric. The purpose is worthy, but the manner is unfortunate. Chapter 5 at least implies that the mock-reader, like the narrator and unlike Mr. Roe, will make just distinctions and evaluations, but Chapter 17 establishes a sharp demarcation between a narrating "I" who desires "you to be in perfect charity" with Mr. Irwine, and that reading "you" who thinks Irwine "was not—as he ought to have been—a living demonstration of the benefits attached to the national church" (1:271, chap. 17). But if the "I" improves the facts, how will "you" learn to "tolerate, pity and love . . . these more or less ugly, stupid, inconsistent people [in the real world] . . . for whom you should cherish all possible hopes, all possible patience" (1:267)? There are several problems with this: it strays too far away for much too long from Mr. Irwine and returns to him only to begin a discussion of the nature of religion; it implies that the facts alone are *not* enough to defend him, even that he might be tainted with stupidity and inconsistency; and it insults the mock-reader, who cannot be expected to admit the numerous deficiencies attributed to him throughout the chapter, or to love a character on orders from an almost hostile narrator.

Fortunately for Irwine as standard, the facts *are* enough to support his final role as judge and peacemaker between Arthur and Adam. In the climactic chapter of Book 5, Irwine fully embodies the ideal of sound moral judgment fused with compassion and pardon. He is present to Adam as mentor and example and thus to the reader as a living measure of Adam's progress. When the two men are alike in mercy, they can join as counsel to the Poysers in their decision to stay and thus restore the social order in Hayslope.

For in the Hayslope world, the center of order *is* the Hall Farm, by far the novel's most important standard for judgment and response.[5] It is the locus of all the values seen partially in other places: honorable social distinctions and obligations at the Donnithorne Chase, devotion and reverence at the church, skillful and honest labor in Burge's shop. All the major characters are assessed by their degree of harmony with these values and made happy to the degree they can finally assimilate them. Adam's development, in particular, is completed by his incorporation into the Poyser family. The rhetorical presentation of the Hall Farm, therefore, will be almost totally sympathetic; but because it is not quite the best of all possible worlds, its defects too should be consistently represented and interpreted.

It must be noted that the Hall Farm is not simply Mrs. Poyser, however much she "keeps at the top o' the talk" (1:359, chap. 21). In plain fact, Mrs. Poyser is not really made to keep her proper distance. How many readers ever think of her as a minor character, which she really is, or find Dinah more interesting than she? Mrs. Poyser has rightly been called the "mouthpiece of the community,"[6] but she alone is not the norm. Rather, she reflects both the best qualities and the one grave flaw to be found in the whole Poyser world.

The narrator dwells with love on the multiple details of this world. Descriptions include everything from fleeces of wool and animal sounds to lists of fruit and flowers; the very riot of fertility and specification enforces awareness of the richness, beauty, and worth of life on this farm. Numerous idiomatic dialogues reflect a camaraderie that seems always warm and amusing, a positive, stabilizing force. Both descriptions and dialogues are often rendered with the elegant diction and wit of a narrator who knows classic culture yet can tenderly appreciate the symbols of rural existence. It is thus implied that the reader should respond with equal appreciation, should approve the Poysers' behavior virtually without question, and should judge very negatively anyone who violates their norms.

The narrator's enthusiasm is hardly qualified by comment or diction until after Hetty's fall. Yet from the start, this attitude jars against evidence that the Hall Farm is an imperfect world, that its people are deeply flawed by severity to those who err.[7] The prime example is the discrepancy between the comic treatment and the facts of Mrs. Poyser's ranting. However well meant, it is not all harmless. For it is leveled not only at the maids and Dinah, who understand the kind heart under it, but constantly at Hetty, who cannot understand. Mrs. Poyser administers this scolding "from her anxiety to do well by her husband's niece—who had no mother of her own to scold her, poor thing!" (1:121, chap. 7); but we are not told of any demonstrations of affection, understanding, or kindly encouragement. Mrs. Poyser never suggests, as Dinah does, that Hetty come to her in trouble; hence in her tragic need, Hetty is alone, and fear of going home drives her to a desperate act. This is not to make Mrs. Poyser into a sinister or cruel woman, but a realization that her tirades are not all praiseworthy entertainment certainly mitigates blame for Hetty's faults and crime and inclines us to favor Adam when he tries to excuse her weakness. Yet there is little evidence of that realization in the narrator before Book 5. George Eliot said she wrote Mrs. Poyser's dialogue "with heightening gusto" (GEL 2:512), and that certainly seems to be the response encouraged in the reader.

It is unfortunate that the rhetoric adjusting our view of the Poysers is not fully consistent, because their fault in abandoning Hetty is crucial to Adam's education, and we should be well prepared for it. In their defect he sees his own (2:214, chap. 42), and his readier conversion to mercy creates much of our final sympathy for him.

The Poysers eventually learn mercy from Adam, but even more so from Dinah. In the rhetoric of the novel, Dinah and the Poysers point the strengths and weaknesses of each other's characters. She has the fund of mercy they lack, partly because she is free of their rather heavy preoccupation with material wants and personal honor. But they have a realism and a hearty, wholesome appreciation of earth's joys, which she undervalues. The reader is thus kept in a balance of sympathy between them. When the Poysers have learned her mercy, they can be reconciled to the sinners; when she has learned their values, she can be fulfilled in love and remain among them. The resolution is both artistically and emotionally satisfying.

Bartle Massey, Lizbeth and Seth Bede, Mr. Irwine and the Poysers—from each we learn something of what the principal characters, especially Adam, must and must not be. As Adam comes to full sympathy with them, eliminating their faults and adopting their virtues in his own character, so we come to full sympathy with him. Seth may be diminished too much, Mr. Irwine defended too much, and the Poysers criticized too late in the novel. Nevertheless, the minor characters are generally successful in directing the reader's right distance from the principals.

The Major Characters

Despite the successful rhetoric of the normative characters, readers have always felt some discomfort with the four principals, usually due to extreme personal differences from them or the narrative handling of their struggles and errors. But the aesthetic validity of the discomfort depends on whether or not the characters are successfully related to the central issue of the novel. Arthur, Hetty, and Dinah must engage our sympathies for Adam's sake; Adam must be interesting and sympathetic on his own. The least problematic of the four is Arthur Donnithorne, generally considered the most successfully distanced.

Arthur is above all Adam's "young squire," his trusted friend, the custodian of his society and his best hopes. In the novel he exists to destroy that trust and those hopes and to be forgiven when Adam learns to love; all his fictional life, therefore, should bear a relation to Adam's moral education so that it will remain the primary object of interest. The reader must be fond of Arthur as Adam is, morally repelled by his actions as Adam is, yet always ahead of Adam in understanding and pardoning his weakness.

Arthur's weakness is personal, but it is realized in a social context. He violates everyone's trust and hopes, a fact that aggravates Adam's revulsion. It is necessary then that he be "placed" in his social context so that the reader may know what are the obligations and values to which he should adhere. Then his distance from the reader can be made commensurate with his own distance from those norms.

Most scenes of Arthur in Books 1 through 3 give him this social placement. He is seen as beloved friend and godson to the Irwines, old friend and present patron to Adam, and a young god to his tenants, who expect from his accession to the estate a "millennial abundance" of improvements (1:124–25, chap. 7). Even in the scenes with Hetty, Arthur is not only a sensual young man but a protecting, patronizing landlord. These scenes function rhetorically to make the reader share the characters' affection for Arthur and also know the strict limits on his possible relationships with them.

The birthday celebration of Book 3 especially serves these purposes. The account may be too long, but the event is needed to guide the reader's judgment before the affair with Hetty reaches its climax. Details like the ringing of the church bells, the arrival of the old people, and the ordering of the dinner tables, seating, and dancing, all reiterate that this is a society with precise hierarchical distinctions and a stable but still viable order of loyalties and honorable dependence stretching over generations. The very scene of Arthur's warmest union with his tenants, the health-drinking, is permeated with evidence of the impenetrable barriers of rank and obligation that divide him from them and prohibit absolutely his marrying one of them. We must feel this enough to be certain that Arthur could never make a successful marriage with Hetty, even aside from her character, and that he is right in his refusal to attempt it. Any illusion about this could obscure his actual and very grave guilt in setting up assignations with a girl to whom he knows he will never be committed but who cannot understand that herself. And it would generate a sort of pity for Hetty that is not due her; she is deceived but not exactly jilted.

Because Arthur, unlike Hetty, really wants to live by the norms and realities of his environment, he is a sympathetic character. He wants to share family affection but cannot get it from his grandfather. He wants to work at managing the estate but is forced to idleness. He wants to treat the tenants fairly but is frustrated by the Old Squire's stinginess. All these factors prepare our understanding of the temptation that causes him to make miserable those whom he would most choose to make happy. Though we share Adam's liking for Arthur as "one o' those gentlemen as wishes to do the right thing" (1:406, chap. 24), and though we know he is weak rather than vicious, still we are alienated from him by the consciousness with which he does the wrong thing. He considers that Hetty's reputation will be injured, that he cannot marry her; he thinks about "those excellent people, the Poysers, to whom a good name was as precious as if they had the best blood in the land in their veins." But he at once reverts to himself—"he should hate himself if he made a scandal of that sort . . . among tenants by whom he liked, above all, to be respected" (1:206, chap. 13). His failure is rooted in an ugly vanity and lack of real concern for others.

Given this background, if we saw Arthur only externally, as Adam and the Poysers see him, we could undergo almost the same shock of unconquerable revulsion against him that they experience. But the crux of the story is Adam's learning to forgive

Arthur, and we must be able to watch that with sympathy, without experiencing the same difficulty Adam has. Therefore the distance between Arthur and the reader must be diminished by an internal view of his struggles, yet without allowing him to usurp the central interest.

When the trouble begins in earnest, the narrator undertakes an analysis of Arthur as he is and as he sees himself:

> Arthur felt himself very heroic as he strode toward the stables. . . . His own approbation was necessary to him, and it was not an approbation to be enjoyed quite gratuitously; it must be won by a fair amount of merit. . . . But he had an agreeable confidence that his faults were all of a generous kind—impetuous, warm-blooded, leonine. . . . It was not possible for Arthur Donnithorne to do anything mean, dastardly, or cruel. "No! I'm a devil of a fellow for getting myself into a hobble, but I always take care the load shall fall on my own shoulders." Unhappily there is no inherent poetical justice in hobbles. . . . (1:184, chap. 12)

Half in and half out of Arthur's mind, the narrator renders the young man's self-image and by partial irony in tone and diction ("felt himself . . . it was not possible") qualifies it. The technique simultaneously provokes sympathetic comprehension and that judgment which prevents identification with his fatuous self-confidence. Similar effects are gained by the subsequent moves all the way into his mind for his debates with himself (chaps. 12, 13, 16). Through these excellent analyses, nearly as good as anything George Eliot was to do later on, we foresee the outcome of Arthur's weakness but are prevented from detesting him as a mere sensual, unprincipled aristocrat deliberately seducing a farm girl.

During the birthday celebration, we are given only glimpses within Arthur, to let us know the incomplete state of the seduction (1:399, chap. 24) and his useless intentions to forego the "flirtation" before it commits him. There are no narrations of the sexual climax of the affair. This reticence serves importantly to diminish our concern with the affair for its own sake. When the evil is completed, we have the long probe of Chapter 29, the morning after the fight with Adam. The glimpses need expansion so that we may know Arthur has not become calloused nor vicious. There must remain something in him to merit Adam's forgiveness.

After Chapter 29, Arthur disappears until Chapter 44, so that the focus may be maintained on Adam's suffering. Arthur is present only in Irwine's reassurances about his character, which the reader already knows. Interest, then, lies in Adam's slow reaction to Arthur through the rector. The representation of Arthur's return is necessary to validate Irwine's statements and Arthur's later mood and interaction with Adam, but it must not allow him belatedly to wrest interest from Adam. Therefore, after his convulsive awakening, Arthur again disappears until his meeting and reconciliation with Adam in Chapter 48.

The emotional power of that scene derives from the interaction of character: Arthur's pleas for compassion overcome Adam's last resistance and elicit a gesture of pardon, which in turn overcomes Arthur's last defensiveness and elicits his full confession. The ''strong rush'' of mutual affection is, as it should be, shared by the reader.

Because this interview is the ultimate and successful test for Adam, it completes the need for Arthur's close presence in the novel. His Epilogue return in ''interesting and picturesque ill-health'' is not really objectionable;[8] it is thematically appropriate that, when fully converted, he be reconstituted in his society; and an anticlimactic refocus is avoided by keeping him offstage.

Blackwood considered Arthur the ''least satisfactory character'' (*GEL*, 2:492). True, he has not the interest of great complexity, and his action is limited and sadly commonplace. But he is thoroughly delineated in himself, from within and without, and the narrator is most in control when dealing with him. Habitually the wise, knowledgeable moralist probes and interprets Arthur without animosity, according to facts, for the benefit of a reader who is treated as wise enough to comprehend and evaluate justly. Most of all, Arthur is kept almost totally within the limits demanded by Adam's centrality. According to the requirements of the novel's form, he seems a successfully distanced character.

Critics of *Adam Bede* have never agreed to grant George Eliot this same success in distancing Hetty Sorrel. Early reviewers praised Hetty's portrait as truthful and consistent; modern critics have often viewed her as the victim of George Eliot's own dislikes and fantasies. Much of the disagreement has flowed, I think, from the failure to distinguish between the conception and the narrative handling of the character and to consider Hetty in relation to the novel as a whole, not as an isolated piece of artistry.

Hetty is a valid conception of a type and of an individual; and in the context of the whole novel she is and must be functionally unsympathetic, because she is disoriented from her proper values—far more so than Arthur—and because Adam must learn genuine love through his deception in her. George Eliot's necessary task, then, was to portray Hetty so as to keep the reader interested in her but relatively detached, to make Adam's infatuation comprehensible and sympathetic yet not make its fulfillment seem desirable, to make Hetty's suffering felt as part of Adam's and sympathy for her felt as part of our sympathy for him, and to make us share Dinah's compassion for Hetty in such a way that love and admiration for Dinah predominate. It was a large order, larger than George Eliot could quite execute at this point in her career.

Nevertheless, some of her techniques were wisely chosen. One is presenting Hetty in regular juxtaposition to Dinah. While Hetty has her first coquettish conversation with Arthur, Dinah has a serious one with Irwine (chaps. 7,8). While Hetty responds indifferently to the Bedes' sorrow, Dinah shows rapid and active concern. From these contrasts we gain initial interest in Hetty but also a justly negative impression of her character. At times the contrast is overdrawn, as by the emotive diction in the scenes of the girls in their bedrooms (chap. 15). But the basic technique is valid and prepares us to see Dinah both save Hetty and replace her.

Another apt technique for negatively distancing Hetty is the lack of dialogue in her representation. Throughout the first four

Books, Hetty speaks only about thirty times, and usually only a Yes, No, or the briefest form of assent, question, or answer. This inarticulateness suits her narrow and introverted mentality, assists in limiting the amount of interest we can take in her for her own sake, and thus keeps her within the bounds of her proper function in the novel.

Though the reader is never to be attracted or deceived by Hetty, he must understand why Adam is. The most obvious reason, of course, is her beauty, which is very adequately represented. But Adam's love is interpreted as more than sexual attraction to beauty, and here Hetty's inarticulateness becomes a problem. Before Arthur's rejection, Hetty and Adam have only two exchanges, in the Hall Farm garden and at the birthday dance; afterward we are told that she begins to talk more in his presence, but never what she says. There is no conversation from which Adam could deduce in her that ''character,'' that desire to do good work and make the world better, which, above all, he admires. That is a delusion he builds from Mrs. Poyser's statements that Hetty is clever at her work (2:5, chap. 27).

With so little dialogue, it really is hard to comprehend so thorough a delusion in an intelligent man. The technique that makes it most nearly acceptable is George Eliot's placement of Hetty firmly in the Poyser world, so that she seems to partake of its vitality and wholesomeness. She is first seen in the rich and delightful dairy (chap.7), also the first place Adam visits at the Hall Farm. He meets her in the garden, full of ripe fruits and flowers, of which she seems to be one. It is understandable that Adam could think her as well adapted to her surroundings as he is himself, since he has not the reader's inside knowledge that ''Hetty's World'' is really an empty dream of luxuries (chap. 9).

The portrayal of Hetty, in short, is satisfactory if we are to admit that Adam's ''sweet delusion'' (1:333, chap. 20) is somewhat surprising and rather foolish, but explicable. If it is to be more than that, then we have another rhetorical problem, which will be examined later in relation to the interpretation of Adam.

Since Hetty really has nothing in herself except prettiness to recommend her, the narrator must sustain the reader's interest in her. And her inability to speak for herself until so late in the novel makes her absolutely dependent on his objectivity for a fair presentation. Here is the heart of the rhetorical problem. For the critics' charges against George Eliot of vindictiveness, condescension, and the like, take their origin and force from the narrator's treatment of Hetty.[9]

At its best, narrative description of Hetty is just, though seldom sympathetic and never without a note of warning. Descriptions of her looks and manner convey truthfully how deceptively appealing she is. Because her thoughts are almost as limited as her words, the narrator supplements them by a fusion of her mind with his own. In the accounts of her notion of Adam (1:145-46, chap. 9), of her reactions to Arthur's attentions (chaps. 9, 13, 15), of her projections of the dismal future after his rejection (2:69, chap. 31), and of her bewildered longing for home (2:124-25, chap. 36), we find specificity of detail, elaborated comparisons, and educated diction that indicate the narrator is supplying what Hetty intuits but could scarcely formulate. We thus derive both an appropriate sympathy for her and a firm assurance that Adam, however he is enticed and deceived, will be far happier without her.

This much is necessary and well accomplished. The great problem arises when the narrator begins a direct attack on Hetty. The trouble appears in the opening description of her in the dairy, with the strangely combined diction about her "beauty like that of kittens or very small downy ducks . . . or babies . . . with which you can never be angry, but that you feel ready to crush for inability to comprehend the state of mind into which it throws you" (1:121, chap. 7). The tolerant narrator has here become either cruel or tangled in his grammar, for he may mean that he wishes to crush not fragile beauty but rather the feeling it rouses in him; the reader, however, may not see any good reason for either impulse.

In Chapter 15 the narrator interrupts Hetty's nighttime preening with a lengthy commentary on her attributes:

Ah, what a prize the man gets who wins a sweet bride like Hetty! How the men envy him . . . . The dear, young, round, soft, flexible thing! Her heart must be just as soft, her temper just as free from angles . . . . the little darling is so fond of him, her little vanities are so bewitching, he wouldn't consent to her being a bit wiser; those kitten-like glances and movements are just what one wants . . . . Nature has written out his bride's character for him in those exquisite lines of cheek and lip and chin, in those eyelids delicate as petals, in those long lashes . . . . How she will dote on her children! . . . and the husband will look on, smiling benignly, able, whenever he chooses, to withdraw into the sanctuary of his wisdom. . . . pray ask yourself . . . if you ever *could* . . . believe evil of the *one* supremely pretty woman who has bewitched you. No: people who love downy peaches are apt not to think of the stone, and sometimes jar their teeth terribly against it. (1:227-29, chap. 15)

The narrative personality projected here is clearly that of an unpleasant, waspish woman who dislikes men and takes satisfaction in their painful awakening from delusion. And the mock-reader is clearly a man, one of the deceived lot who will deserve what they get. But the whole passage is really unfair, to Hetty in its nagging insistence on her deceptive features and moral deficiencies, to both pretty women and men in its generalized implication that the former are infantile and the latter arrogant and stupid. And when the narrator says that "it was very much in this way that our friend Adam Bede thought about Hetty," there is no use in further counseling us not to consider him "deficient in penetration" because "the wisest of us," "I" for instance, are similarly fooled (1:229).

Bad enough as a biting woman, the narrator next turns prosecutor, putting Hetty on trial before her time: "Does any sweet or sad memory mingle with this dream of the future—any loving thought of her second parents—of the children she had helped to tend—of any youthful companion, any pet animal, any relic of her own childhood even? Not one" (1:230). The long passage goes on and on, arraying the evidence that Hetty "had no feeling at all" for any part of the Hall Farm or any of its people. But it all backfires on its purpose, which, as a matter of fact, is a good one. We *ought* to know Hetty's flaws well, *ought* to be safely distanced from her, but this verbal castigation stirs an irrational sympathy for the "picked-on" character, an assumption that she cannot be *that bad*. The mock-reader is clearly expected to be at one with the narrator in sentiment and opinion, but here, if anywhere in George Eliot's work, is presupposed a mock-reader we refuse to become.

Had the narrator's aggressive tactics worked, we would all but despise this girl. Perhaps George Eliot felt this likelihood and endeavored to compensate by the detailed accounts of her misery. She may have overcompensated.

Improved narrative methods appear as soon as Hetty's dreams have collapsed. After her reading of Arthur's letter, the narrator offers a close analysis of her shock and despair in a tone of restrained pity, with wise generalizations from human experience (2:66-71, chap. 31). From now on, in this tragedy that is too big for her to comprehend or cope with, Hetty's sorrows will often be linked narratively to those of her fellow mortals (chaps. 35, 36). She is incapable of any breadth of vision or feeling for others, but in this universal context we can feel for her pain without being engrossed by it.

There can be little doubt that the two chapters of Hetty's journey (chaps. 36, 37) are *in themselves* some of the best portrayal of character and event in the novel, powerfully effective for reducing the unsympathetic distance between Hetty and the reader. Comment is reduced to a minimum; we are isolated with the solitary girl, forced to share her repulsion from crass onlookers—the jocose coachman, the drunken, hilarious postilion, and the staring, lounging men in public houses. We enter deeply into her experience through George Eliot's depiction of small, telling actions—her fixing on one tree after another as a goal to be reached on the road, her plea for sixpence change from her last shilling, her delay in suicide, since "there was all the night to drown herself in" (2:147, chap. 37), her kissing her own arms in the sheer joy of being still alive. In this episode of the attempted suicide, George Eliot came very close to stream-of-consciousness; distance is annihilated and we are unbearably enclosed in Hetty's tormented brain.

It is no wonder, then, that critics and students in such numbers have insisted that Hetty is the central character and more interesting than any other. It is this representation of her futile dragging after Arthur that chiefly produces this effect, and therefore one is forced to question whether these obviously well-done chapters are not too elaborated for Hetty's function in the whole novel. At this point, it is thematically necessary that she depart from the center of social values, the Hall Farm, and the narrator must show her solitude as finally desperate enough to permit her to murder her child. We need enough detail for genuine sympathy—but no more, for our sympathy must be qualified by a felt artistic demand for the completion of her tragic downfall, moderated enough to make a practical interest in Adam's reactions paramount. But in fact, the journey becomes our point of highest practical concern for Hetty's human safety and happiness. Furthermore, the elaborated account of the journey has little inherent link to the rest of the story; no other character ever knows its details or mentions it except as part of Hetty's general misery. It does not affect another character's reaction to her in any specific manner, and consequently does not influence the reader's reaction to the character. It only creates an absorbing fascination with the suffering girl for her own sake—which ought not to be.

Fortunately for the novel's focus, Hetty is moved offstage from the last lap of the journey until the prison scene (except as others see her in the courtroom). During this time, our focus must be on Adam, our viewpoint his. Through Irwine, Bartle Massey, and Adam himself, we hear all we need of Hetty, enough, perhaps too much, for our proper sympathy with Adam.

The prison scene could have aggravated the problem created by the journey, but here the distancing is more successful in relation to the needs and proportions of the novel. In Hetty's confession the emphasis is on her bewildered and desperate motives, and the psychological realism definitely softens our judgment. Yet Dinah's presence and words keep us conscious of the crime as a crime, so that Hetty gets only the benefit that her own fears and confusion can give her. The scene's primary stress is, as it should be, on the power of Dinah's love, so soon to be crucial to Adam's future.

Hetty has one final task in her artistic life, to ask Adam to forgive her and to tell Arthur that, at Dinah's urging, she is trying to forgive him. Though pity for Hetty runs high in this scene, the attention is still focused on Adam's anguish and on his first great act of pardon. In these last links to Adam and to Dinah, Hetty has, in effect, prepared her successor and can drop out of the novel.

But many of George Eliot's readers have accepted that successor only with reluctance and under protest—a fact that irritated the author herself, who noted in her *Journal*, "The *Saturday* criticism is characteristic: Dinah is not mentioned!" Yet she was meant to be the "principal figure at the last" (*GEL*, 2:503). If George Eliot meant Dinah to be the principal figure at any point, she temporarily lost sight of her own scheme; Dinah, first to last, exists primarily for Adam, to give him an abiding example of love toward the frail and erring, to strengthen him in sorrow, to learn from him that a full love embraces joy, and thus, by her love, to bring his to completion. To be distanced properly for her role, therefore, Dinah must be vivified and appealing as a standard of love, a corrective to others, yet distanced by her narrowness and need of enlightenment. Both her virtues and her deficiencies must be noted from the beginning. Though subordinated in the early events, she must be sufficiently present that a reader will never lose sight of her importance and will pick up the signals of the final outcome of her love. She must be in some way active on Adam's behalf throughout the novel so that the end may be prepared and convincing.

The objections to Dinah as a character idealized out of reality are not without due cause. Yet if we look at Dinah in herself, we find an accurate and interesting conception, a girl from a harsh mill town, poor, with less of weight or coloring than her country cousins, but pretty and capable of a strong personal love, which a rather fanatical doctrine has converted wholly into compassion for sin and suffering but which she is to learn to trust and to develop in a balanced, integrated life. The primary obstacle to the vivifying and individualizing of this conception is that George Eliot does not seem fully able to recognize Dinah's deficiencies for what they are, to see that Dinah has suppressed her own vitality, or to create a rhetoric that will both criticize her for that and rouse the reader's eager expectation of the fulfillment of her true potential.

A large part of the problem is located in the rhetoric of diction. Dinah's own has a distancing effect, due less, perhaps, to its suggestion of sanctimoniousness in her than to the mere quantity of indirect biblical quotation and sectarian phraseology:

> Doubtless it is so sometimes; for there have been evil-doers among us who have sought to deceive the brethren, and some there are who deceive their own selves. But we are not without discipline and correction to put a check upon these things. There's a very strict order kept among us, and the brethren and sisters watch for each other's souls as they that must give account. They don't go every one his own way and say, ''Am I my brother's keeper?'' (1:130-31, chap. 8)

This sort of thing appears in much of her dialogue, in the narrative accounts of her thought, and profusely in her letter. However true to her type it may be, the sheer quantity of it causes the individual character to escape us for lack of enough personally distinguishing speech. But that it is not merely the religious content causing the trouble is indicated by the difference in the first part of her sermon:

> Why, you and me, dear friends, are poor. We have been brought up in poor cottages, and have been reared on oat-cake, and lived coarse. . . . We are just the sort of people that want to hear good news. . . . But perhaps doubts come into your mind like this: Can God take much notice of us poor

people? . . . how do we know he cares for us any more than we care for the worms and things in the garden, so as we rear our carrots and onions? (1:33-34, chap. 2)

Here the diction and phraseology are simple, direct, homely—her own speech as a common woman; much of the charm of this part of the sermon and the sympathy it wins for Dinah flow from the language and the simple human feeling here displayed. Since this idiom could have given some of the appeal Dinah needs, it seems too bad George Eliot did not make a more consistent use of it.

A case could be made that Dinah's sectarian diction is an accurate reflection of the unhealthy limitations she has placed on her personal development and emotional expression in the first part of the novel. In that case, we might expect that the narrator's own diction would suggest this interpretation and would help us discover the real, living woman. But the narrator's diction makes Dinah even less vital than her own and hints of no awareness of her deficiencies.

The descriptions of Dinah simply smother the human girl under ill-chosen rhetoric. Her eyes are "loving, grave, simple, candid," and *always* "mild"; her face is perpetually "calm, grave, gentle, serene" and "pale." These repeated adjectives finally suggest a blank immobility, which suggestion is certainly not offset by the analogies to "a lovely corpse" (1:238, chap. 15) and an angel sitting on a grave (1:162, chap. 10). Nor do the descriptions of her mental, emotional life suggest her real complexity or potential. Her "pure and tender mind" is always filled with "rapid thought and noble impulse," "benignant hopefulness," "deep concentrated calmness," and "sad, yearning love."

The trouble is that these descriptions, though sometimes almost laughable, betray no scrap of humor or irony in the narrator. They all appear in episodes where Dinah's acts or conversation are clearly meant to win the fullest approval and sympathy for her and not at all to point her limitations. The adjectives clearly intend highly favorable connotations and thus are interpretive as well as descriptive. And some, as in "thrilling treble" (1:133, chap. 8), describe not Dinah but the desired response: if you are not thrilled like her audience, you must be dull. In general, the narrator's diction implies that Dinah's character is nearly perfect, a judgment not well supported by all the facts in the first fifteen chapters.

Dinah's limitations, represented in her actions and dialogue, form a counter-rhetoric to the narrative idealization. She is narrow in her views of life and religion. She fails to note that religion in ''high-walled streets'' can be the only excitement in a hard life and so tends to identify hard living and excited response with religion (1:134, chap. 8). These views narrow her discernment of others' characters. Her address during her sermon to ''big soft-hearted'' Sandy Jim, ''who was now holding the baby to relieve his wife'' (1:38, chap. 2), generates in the reader a humorous detachment from her concern for sinners by implying that she does not know how to identify them. The same can be said of her assumptions that Bessy Cranage's earrings must be ''dragging [her] down into a dark bottomless pit'' (1:42), that Irwine must have been a ''worldly Sadducee'' (1:137, chap. 8), or that Hetty's nervous tears are a sign of ''the stirring of a divine impulse (1:240, chap. 15). Finally, Dinah is limited in her view of her own character and role. She does not see that her preoccupation with ''all the anguish of the children of men'' (2:59, chap. 30) and her dedication to the suffering, to the exclusion of all personal joy or sorrow, are imbalances in her personality and even hinder her mission to any who happen to be contented.

The use of Mrs. Poyser to criticize Dinah's views is certainly a deliberate technique, but its effect is limited in two ways. For one thing, when Mrs. Poyser snaps at Dinah, ''you look like the statty o' the outside o' Treddles'on church, a-starin' and a-smilin' whether it's fair weather or foul'' (1:115, chap. 6), this analogy mainly affords the reader relief not from Dinah's perfection, but from the narrator's descriptions. Also, in their relationship Mrs. Poyser is more corrected than correcting. She is accurate and amusing in her pungent comments on Dinah's preference for misery, but she proposes an alternative in symbols, not of joy and love fulfilled, but of good food and furnishings. It is really Dinah who teaches Mrs. Poyser to love, and she emerges from their arguments with the edge on the reader's sympathy.

If Dinah's limitations were presented with a better rhetoric, they would bother readers less, for we would be sure she would get over them. Then we would be readier to respond to those qualities of tact, patience, and affection which make her a positive standard in the novel. Her visits to Lisbeth Bede and Hetty, in which she most displays these traits, are events that clearly and justly constitute a rhetoric in her favor.

The prison episode, especially, may be said to rescue Dinah as well as Hetty. The love and psychological finesse with which she approaches Hetty more than compensate for any earlier overdistancing sanctimony and cause us to sympathize with her as never before. It is true that the rhetoric of her prayer would daze anyone as stupefied with suffering as Hetty. Nevertheless, except for the prayer, Dinah's speech is as natural as in the first part of her sermon; and even in the prayer, it is the force of her love and urgency that breaks Hetty's emotional barrier and gives Dinah the success with her in which we are now taking a very strong interest.

The prison scene and Dinah's visit to Adam stimulate a warm, practical interest in her and sense of fitness that Adam should love her. The question remains whether her own awakening to love and to acceptance of it is made credible by adequate preparation and dramatization.

After reading only the first installment sent him, Blackwood intuited the outcome (*GEL*, 2: 446), and probably most other readers do the same. The reason may be that George Eliot wisely structured the rhetoric of events to bring Dinah quickly into Adam's home and to have them meet there in direct and personal confrontation, rather than in the crowded and talkative atmosphere of the Poysers. Also, Dinah's assistance to Adam in relieving and comforting Lisbeth relates her closely to the first major episode of his education and suggests that he could easily become permanently and deeply attracted to her.

Only three suggestions of Dinah's inclination toward Adam

are given prior to Book 6 (1:173, chap. 11; 1:212, chap. 14; 2:254, chap. 46), but its motive is fully there—simple, feminine attraction to a man good, intelligent, and strongly masculine. Here is a woman, not a ''gentle seraph,'' and her first blush does more to put us in tune with her than everything prior to it. But then she is physically absent from Chapter 15 to Chapter 45. Her letter in Chapter 30 is stilted, pietistic, and uninformative, and at best could hardly generate enough interest in her to compete with the violent events to follow. The preparation is right in kind, but it lapses too much in the middle, especially since Hetty is allowed to capture too strong an interest and Dinah is already overdistanced by the other flaws already discussed.

Book 6, however, is beautifully handled. Dinah is thoroughly appealing in her turmoil of emotion, loving but not knowing she is loved, ''beginning to hunger after an equal love'' (2:334, chap. 52) yet paralyzed with fear lest this mean a rejection of the Redeemer. This latter is no small problem to a woman who has lived as she has, and we are meant to feel it. Her love is made to seem a natural development by the repetition of her previous reactions to Adam. She is blushing and self-conscious in his presence, and attracted to his strength by its contrast to the mild timidity of Seth. A low-keyed comedy makes us enter into her feelings with enjoyment: Adam's determined acceptance of her oft-asserted religious dedication is a kind of whimsical pay-off for her lack of self-knowledge; and her comment on Esau is not at all about Arthur, as she thinks it is, but is a subconscious revelation of her preference for the strong man. Shrewd old Lisbeth has just the convincing statement: ''happen, thee'dst like a husband better as isna just the cut o' thysen: the runnin' brook isna athirst for th' rain'' (2:313, chap. 51).

It is credible, then, that Dinah should love Adam, and we can feel for her in her days of uncertainty about his love. But we are not allowed to see her outgrowing her scruples about her right to accept his love.[10] If Dinah was to be anywhere near the ''principal figure at the last,'' if ultimately we were to give her more love and sympathy than Hetty, then surely her inner drama ought to have been staged at least as fully as Hetty's journey. Readers have often felt there is too much of Dinah; perhaps, in truth, there is too little.

Critics have generally refused to share Dinah's admiring love for Adam. Seldom has any fictional character been subjected to such a barrage of name-calling: "a sententious, loquacious prig"; "a walking shadow, a garrulous embodiment of qualities [George Eliot] is resolved to admire"; "a tactless and rough-handed moralist, hard, insensitive, unresponsive to the feelings of the people around him."[11] But it has already been said that Adam is meant to be flawed by his harshness and moralistic severity until love and suffering correct him. The suitable distancing of Adam must, then, retain sympathy for him while he himself learns to feel sympathy; and it must make his process of change and consequent happiness both credible and a matter of intense and primary interest throughout the novel.

The first requirement, sympathy for Adam himself, is made difficult by the general unpleasantness of his particular fault. A reader therefore needs the assistance of a rhetoric of other characters who know Adam and see both his flaws and his redeeming qualities. Should their perception be deficient, this fact should be implied through the narrator's viewpoint.

Yet one questions whether anyone in the novel really recognizes the degree and significance of Adam's intolerable rigidity. The Poysers, Dinah, Arthur, and, until the trial, Irwine, all give him unmitigated admiration. Lisbeth witnesses to his fault against his father, as has been said, but her complaints at his being "so stiff and masterful" (1:180, chap. 11) are neutralized by the annoyance of her whining. Only Bartle Massey seems to have a relation to Adam with which we can identify, and he is seen only twice before Book 5.

We do, of course, identify fairly often with the narrator's view of Adam—often, but not always. The narrator sees Adam's hardness and acknowledges it in a long thematic statement (1:316, chap. 19), yet he at once overcompensates by a long hortative plea to the reader to appreciate this man and his unique worth:

"Look at Adam through the rest of the day . . . . Look at this broad-shouldered man with the bare muscular arms, and the thick firm black hair . . . and with the strong barytone voice bursting every now and then into loud and solemn psalm-tunes, as if seeking an outlet for superfluous strength . . . " (1:318-19). Though the narrator proceeds to disavow any romantic generalizations about peasants, he yet speaks of this one in tones reminiscent of Goldsmith or Gray. The fact is that his admiration for Adam's "faculties trained in skilful courageous labour" (1: 321) so heavily outweighs his deprecation of Adam's defect that he almost seems to interpret the latter as a minor passing ailment.

While Adam is learning humble compassion, the reader's rapport with him is sustained by the evidence of his redeeming capacity for love and gentleness. This capacity is concretized by some event or piece of dialogue with all the characters: his silent endurance of Lisbeth's cruelly ill-judged remarks after Thias's death (1:159, chap. 10), his genuine, unpatronizing love for Seth and his effort to overcome Lisbeth's bias for himself, his respectful gratitude for Dinah's charity, and his deep affection for Arthur, demonstrated enough to convince us that loss of esteem is a chief part of his suffering, as much as jealousy. Equally appealing to us are Adam's relations to the social entities: Burge's shop, Massey's school, and above all, the Poyser farm; in all of them he shows his perfect orientation to the values of labor, family, and friendship.

But one relationship of Adam's creates a special need for sympathy, his love for the vapid, light-minded Hetty. We have already seen that the representation of Hetty makes this love credible as a surprising but comprehensible delusion. The representation of Adam cannot make it more than that and should not make it less. It should not, for instance, be mere stupid infatuation. This problem is reasonably well solved by rendering the external inducements through Adam's viewpoint, especially Hetty's blushing reaction to his approach in the Hall Garden (1:330, chap. 20), her dressing in Dinah's cap to tease him—just the sort of trick pulled by a girl falling in love with a man she has always known (1:342-43)—and her enticing behavior after Arthur's departure (2:96, chap. 33). Though these evidences are a slight basis for love, they account convincingly enough for his deception, provided we can admit that even sensible, admirable Adam could be a bit foolish.

Through most of the story, the narration does not prevent this interpretation. The positive pressure is on Adam's personal traits and workmanship; his love is treated chiefly by a representation of his thoughts. But in Chapter 33 the narrator launches into a two-page comment designed to force our admission that Adam's passion is not merely explicable but admirable and even exalted:

> Possibly you think that Adam was not at all sagacious in his interpretations, and that it was altogether extremely unbecoming in a sensible man to behave as he did . . . . Of course, I know that, as a rule, sensible men fall in love with the most sensible women of their acquaintance . . . . But even to this rule an exception will occur now and then in the lapse of centuries, and my friend Adam was one. For my own part, however, I respect him none the less: nay, I think the deep love he had for that sweet, rounded, blossom-like, dark-eyed Hetty . . . came out of the very strength of his nature, and not out of any inconsistent weakness. Is it any weakness, pray, to be wrought on by exquisite music . . . ? If not, then neither is it a weakness to be so wrought upon by the exquisite curves of a woman's cheek . . . . Beauty has an expression beyond and far above the one woman's soul . . . it is more than a woman's love that moves us in a woman's eyes—it seems to be a far-off mighty love that has come near to us . . . the rounded neck, the dimpled arm, move us by . . . their close kinship with all we have known of tenderness and peace. The noblest nature sees the most of this *impersonal* expression in beauty. . . . (2:96-98)

Such a nature, we are then told, was Adam's, and such his noble emotions.

This passage draws from Ludwig Feuerbach's religion of humanity, in which God is the idea of human perfection, the sum of the highest attributes of our species. One person represents these divine qualities for another and thus becomes the object of a worship imbued with the noblest religious emotion.[12] Such a person, in this passage, is Hetty for Adam.

But Hetty simply cannot credibly sustain such a role. Indeed, the narrator admits her deficiencies, has consistently belabored them in previous passages. Yet he still tries to validate Adam's emotion as suitable and noble. The attempt is undercut by the stress only on Hetty's qualities that are strictly physical and sexually enticing—dark eyes, dimples, and curves. Such a girl might arouse passion and even a deception about the hollow under her lovely surface. But to insist that she could touch "the spring of all love and tenderness, all faith and courage" is to make Adam look not less but more foolish.

As if the narrator realized the weakness of his argument, he insists upon it the more aggressively. The passage is another alienating essay, marred by tasteless irony and the renewed implication that "you," the reader, are unable or unwilling to understand "my friend Adam" whom "for my own part, however, I respect," presumably because "I" can appreciate the finest effects of beauty on the spirit. Once the narrator demanded that the mock-reader make too little of Hetty; now he insists on making too much of her in order to make much of Adam. In both cases he stands to lose the real reader.

Without this passage and its echoes elsewhere, we could accept Adam's misguided love for Hetty, but it is harder to pity his error of assuming that she can love him. He seems to presume that he need only maintain his customary righteousness and he is sure to win her. His total failure to see that he cannot touch her kind of desire is the probable reason why we, like Blackwood, find ourselves unable to feel very sorry for him when he discovers her with Arthur (*GEL*, 2:484).

However, we are obviously intended to feel sorry. The moment of discovery is preceded by a leisurely account of Adam's happy thoughts about Hetty, Arthur, his work, and his prospects from all three. The irony, intensified by the slow pace, is meant to prepare fellow-feeling with Adam's shock, which in turn will prepare for the total convulsion of pain when he is totally undeceived by Irwine's news.

Blackwood correctly predicted that "sympathies will gather round him keenly when the full force of his affliction comes upon him and the tender and stern fibres in his heart of oak fairly begin to struggle" (*GEL*, 2:484). In the scenes of his grief, emotional distance shrinks. But one must still ask if it shrinks enough, given the centrality of this character and of his conversion through grief.

Because Adam's character has been so rigid and static till this point, a reader needs much evidence of the anguish that is powerful enough to change him radically. And much is provided. The rhetoric of events and dialogue is highly effective in the scenes with Seth and Irwine, in the upper room, and at the trial. Adam's condition is made psychologically convincing and intensely sympathetic especially by the use of vivid details: his sense of bewildered alienation from his workshop (2:167, chap. 38), his collapse into sobs on Seth's neck (168), the violent, resistant gestures and sharp phrases with which he reacts to Irwine's breaking the news (2:181, chap. 39), his refusal to hear any proofs of guilt before the trial (2:208, chap. 42), and especially the anguished phrases that reveal the center point of his grief: "My poor Hetty . . . I thought she loved me . . . and was good" (2:203-4, chap. 41).

Nevertheless, one cannot flatly deny the statement that Adam's suffering "does not possess and haunt the reader's imagination as Hetty's does."[13] Given the detailed presentation of Adam's grief, it is likely that this is yet another effect of the over-dramatization of Hetty's journey. By the time we see Adam's anguish, we have already been engrossed in Hetty's. His excruciating instruction is conducted chiefly through news and conversation about her, so that every secondhand account accentuates the compassion we have already felt for her. Thus we are concerned for her too much as Adam is—with overwhelming pity for her, which is his role, rather than for him, which is ours.

In the long run, sympathy with Adam is most promoted by his own growing awareness of and will to correct his besetting defect.

This growth begins with his self-accusation at Thias's funeral. It proceeds as he finds in himself, first, new weakness requiring support from Irwine, Massey, and Dinah, and then new compassion for Martin Poyser, Hetty, all who "have suffered like this" (2:210, chap. 42), and, finally, Arthur. Each advance is marked by a confession, and each confession, of course, increases the reader's sympathy with Adam; ours grows in proportion to his.

The final outcome of Adam's change of heart, his love for Dinah, ought to be as credible and interesting as his first love, since it is destined to succeed, yet it presents considerable difficulty. Before Book 6, there is even less preparation of his love for her than of hers for him. We are given only his interest in her for Seth's sake (1:173, 181, chap. 11), his strong memory of her looks and voice (2:62, chap. 30), and his gratitude for her mercy to Hetty (2:254, chap. 46). Their interview after the trial helps to account for the love, but does not certainly forewarn of it.

As Book 6 unfolds, the narrator's accounts of Adam's psychological preparation for new love (2:303-4, chap. 50) and of his inward reactions to sudden recognition of it (2:324, chap. 51) are convincing, as are Adam's reflections on his past sorrow and present joyous love (chaps. 53, 54). But what most convinces and most invites our participation is Lisbeth's discernment and insistence (chap. 51). The rich humor of her speech, nearly as salty as Mrs. Poyser's, and the joke in "acute" Adam's having to learn his own mind from her, create an immediate belief and rapport with all concerned. We accept what amuses and delights us.

Yet it remains questionable whether the reader ought to be so dependent for his belief on the narrator and Lisbeth, instead of on a visible and dramatized development of Adam's love. This need not be a long drama, since the crux of the novel is Adam's learning *how* to love. But he is still learning until he knows *where* he can love best, and with so much of this action occurring offstage, indeed, even out of his conscious thought, the long, vivid picture of his love for Hetty remains so engrossing that the second love can hardly compete.

This is true in terms of length of treatment, but even more so in terms of Dinah's personality and change. She simply is not "felt" enough, for the reasons already explored, and consequently the force of Adam's attraction to her and their mutual alteration, love, and happiness cannot be felt enough either. The drama pleases and wins our notional assent, but it fails to absorb as, by its thematic importance, it should.

It is noticeable that those events in *Adam Bede* which do engross are the most external in character: the scenes at Poysers, the birthday events, the encounters of Hetty, Arthur, and Adam in the woods, Hetty's journey, and the scenes in Adam's upper room and Hetty's cell. George Eliot, in this her first novel, had not yet learned to make mental events compellingly interesting and impressive. She had found one important tool in the use of the small, revealing, external detail, but for the most part she still relied on the explanations of the narrator. In time, she would make narrative analysis a brilliant success, as fully engaging as the dramatized scene, but at this stage, her narrator was too often in a fluctuating, unbalanced, or even unwarranted relation to the characters and to the reader. Therefore the reader's distance from the characters is often fluctuating, out of line with what the total pattern requires and the author obviously wished.

As she developed the technique of analysis, George Eliot also increased the level of psychological complexity she could create. The characters in *Adam Bede* are, for the most part, accurately conceived, but they are not very complex. Because they are readily comprehended, intellectual interest can be exhausted. Without the need for a regularly reconsidered and deepened response, the reader cannot offer very deep or prolonged sympathy.

But the successes of *Adam Bede* far outweigh its defects and prevail over narrator's mistakes and reader's aloofness. At its completion George Eliot wondered if she would "ever write another book as true as 'Adam Bede.' "[14] The novel is not "true" in all respects; though the characters are represented truthfully, they are not always interpreted accurately. And George Eliot would write several books more true. But the validity of her basic perceptions, feeling, and technique in *Adam Bede* makes it a powerful forecast of the greatness yet to come.

Notes

1. E. S. Dallas, *The Times*, 12 April 1859, reprinted in *George Eliot and Her Readers*, ed. John Holstrom and Laurence Lerner (New York: Barnes and Noble, Inc., 1966), p. 19.

2. I refrain from repeating or documenting the abundant argument over the happy ending. I do stand with its defenders and say that the love Adam learns must fasten onto someone. Also, the comic thrust in presenting the Poysers has gone too far to permit a final, tragic destruction of their happiness. The artistic problem with the happy ending lies not in its formal fitness but in the preparation of our responses to the characters involved. Of this, more later.

3. These two events are explicitly related in a long thematic passage that defines Adam's weakness, his need for a ''long and hard lesson'' in sharing the suffering of guilty loved ones, and the function of his father's death as the ''alphabet'' of that lesson. The formal unity of the book would be discoverable without this passage; with it, the intended unity is undeniable. George Eliot, *Adam Bede*, Standard Edition in 2 vols. (Edinburgh: William Blackwood and Sons, 189-?), 1: 316, chap. 19. This and future citations within the text refer first to volume and page numbers in this edition. For the convenience of users of other editions, chapter numbers are added. When whole chapters are referred to, the citation will so indicate.

4. Cf. John S. Diekhoff, ''The Happy Ending of *Adam Bede*,'' *ELH* 3 (1936): 227.

5. The evaluating function of the Hall Farm is also analyzed by Barbara Hardy, *The Novels of George Eliot* (London: University of London, The Athlone Press, 1959), pp. 185-86, and Dorothy Van Ghent, *The English Novel: Form and Function* (New York: Harper and Row, Torchbooks, 1961), pp. 175-87.

6. W. J. Harvey, *The Art of George Eliot* (New York: Oxford University Press, 1962), p. 157.

7. Cf. the opinion of George H. Creeger, ''An Interpretation of *Adam Bede*,'' *ELH* 23 (1956): 224-25. I cannot agree with him that only Martin Poyser and not his wife represents the flaw of hardness.

8. Cf. Van Ghent, pp. 180-81.

9. Cf. Harvey, p. 87 for an excellent general analysis of the problem. As far as I know, Harvey, pp. 76-77, offers the only specific discussion of the narrative treatment of Hetty in relation to the total pattern. I believe his observations can be carried further and partially challenged.

10. See Creeger, p. 237.

11. Walter Allen, *George Eliot* (New York: Macmillan Co., 1964), p. 103; Gerald Bullett, *George Eliot: Her Life and Books* (London: Collins Press, 1947), p. 171; Jerome Thale, *The Novels of George Eliot* (New York: Columbia University Press, 1959), p. 25.

12. Bernard Paris, *Experiments in Life: George Eliot's Quest for Values* (Detroit, Mich.: Wayne State University Press, 1965), chap. 5, explicates Feuerbach's philosophy and George Eliot's application of it.

13. Neil Roberts, *George Eliot: Her Beliefs and Her Art* (Pittsburgh, Pa.: University of Pittsburgh Press, 1975), p. 71.

14. John Walter Cross, *George Eliot's Life As Related in Her Letters and Journals*, 3 vols. (Boston: Houghton Mifflin Co., 1909), 2:124.

The Mill on the Floss

> The author, midway in her work, has stopped
> to criticize it and to explain her intention to the
> notice of all who wish to understand. . . . She
> says in effect:—''You, reader, are oppressed by
> all this meanness—disgusted at all this hard-
> ness. . . . I perfectly agree with you; but such is
> life, and it is in the midst of such a life . . . that
> my little heroine, Maggie, bloomed into beauty.[1]

Thus did E. S. Dallas, reviewing *The Mill on the Floss*,
paraphrase an important passage at the opening of Book 4. The
actual text of the passage reveals one striking difference:

> I share with you this sense of oppressive narrowness; but it is
> necessary that we should feel it, if we care to understand how it
> acted on the lives of *Tom and Maggie*—how it has acted on
> young natures in many generations. . . . The suffering,
> whether of martyr or victim, which belongs to every historical
> advance of mankind, is represented in this way in every
> town. . . .[2] (Italics added)

Dallas's assumption that the author's central interest was Maggie
Tulliver alone is common, but George Eliot's actual words seem
to state explicitly that her purpose is the revelation of two protagonists, one a martyr and one a victim.

In one reading, then, the story is Maggie Tulliver's. Her family
and suitors have a degree of importance approximately equal to
the span of the book they occupy. Tom, in this reading, is most

important in the early, longest section, but he decreases in importance as he becomes much less present in the last two Books.

The notion of Tom as joint protagonist, however, is supported by his predominance in the long Book 2 and by the six chapters (25, 26, 34, 38, 44, 51) devoted to his rise in business, an experience in which Maggie has no direct part. The twice-used motto ''In their death they were not divided,'' and the repeated parallels and contrasts of Maggie and Tom all suggest that he is not merely her foil but is parallel to her in thematic and structural importance.

Yet neither reading seems to point the focus or to do full justice to all the elements in the book, for Tom is clearly far more important *throughout* Maggie's life than anyone else, yet he cannot compete on equal terms with her, either in the interest of his own personality or in the interest of the fictional pattern of his life. And despite George Eliot's earnest insistence that ''Tom is painted with as much love and pity as Maggie'' and that ''the exhibition of the *right* on both sides was the very soul of my intention'' (*GEL*, 3: 299, 397), she must have known she could not make him as sympathetic as her heroine. In any case, she did not.

The formal focus of the novel, then, the what-it's-about, seems to be this: it is essentially the story of Maggie Tulliver's tragic failure to become a whole and fulfilled woman, despite great intellectual and emotional potential. The failure is due to her inability either to adapt freely to her society's mores and win its approval or to reject those mores and choose her own path out of her own inner freedom and security.[3] Her brother, Tom, is more in this story than anyone else because he is the chief cause of her psychic destruction and reflects it in his own personality. He too is destroyed, as Philip Wakem and Stephen Guest are not (this does not refer to his drowning). Part of Maggie's problem is that she is predominantly ''Sister Maggie'';[4] she always turns to Tom for salvation, turns compulsively, and he cannot provide it because he himself is a damaged and unfree person.[5]

But one must immediately recognize critical divergence from this definition of the whole. Some contend that Maggie's life is not a psychological tragedy but a journey through trial and error toward ultimate maturity, in which Tom shares in his life's final moments.[6] George Eliot's own rhetorical interpretation seems to say this: no matter how bleak the future of the girl who burns Stephen's letter, she is at last spiritually wise and valiant. On a simple human level, it is indeed tragic that such potential cannot be fulfilled in such a crass society; but the tragedy is redeemed by Maggie's ''spiritual'' development, which makes her more a willing martyr than a victim.

This reader can only say that Maggie's final actions do not seem to represent a choice issuing from mature reflection on real alternatives and resulting in inner peace. She has struggled mightily, suffered intensely, and achieved a form of self-conquest, true; but she remains fundamentally compulsive and insecure. In a final ''cry of self-despair'' she herself recognizes the probability that she will ''struggle and fall and repent again'' (2: 391, chap. 58). And nothing in her character development would prevent it.

The previous paragraphs say, in essence, that the story George Eliot meant to tell and tried to make convincing is not exactly the story she did tell—very convincingly. To state the problem another way, Maggie's illustrative and representational roles are in conflict, and a resultant discrepancy can be expected in the rhetoric. She is meant to illustrate the social victim redeemed and ennobled as a person and changed to a willing martyr; for that, the rhetoric should—and usually does—glorify her and invite maximum reduction of distance. But represented facts show a tragically stunted personality, a girl damaged beyond repair, *not* spiritually wise or psychically sound, to be greatly pitied but not glorified.

In Maggie's real tragedy as represented, her proper distancing requires a balanced representation of her admirable qualities and her defects, together with a most sensitive and also firm, intelligent narrative interpretation, so that sympathy does not degenerate into sentimentality. Other characters must be sympathetic in the degree that they promote or impede her fulfillment. When their hindering her is due to their being similarly hindered in their growth (the case with Tom), the sympathy they draw to themselves should aid our understanding and pity for her also. The events of the novel must relate directly, or not too indirectly, to the issue of Maggie's personal development, and they must be elaborated in proportion to their importance in that process. Tom in particular must be presented with the fullness due to the first figure *after* the protagonist, the one most closely associated with her happiness or misery (much as a husband-to-be is presented in a novel of which the bride-to-be is sole center—Knightley in *Emma*, for instance).

If this is an adequate and defensible statement of the formal whole of the novel and its resultant distancing requirements, then it is understandable why that form is obscure to first thoughts and why so many elements of the novel have generated volumes of critical contention. The obscurity of the central meaning results chiefly from a conflict between the rhetoric of events and the rhetoric of narrative voice. Not all the characters are subordinated to their role in Maggie's life; some develop too independently. Some events are overarticulated without adequate purpose; some are suggested as important yet left undeveloped; and some lack clear or credible meaning (alas, the infamous drowning!). And George Eliot herself began the long history of regret over the structure, the "want of proportionate fullness" in the last third of the novel, proportionate, that is, to the "*epische Breite*" of the childhood Books (*GEL*, 3: 317). These problems just listed are found in all parts of the novel, but in the first Books the narrator is clearly aware of the facts; representation and interpretation are more harmonious, and the total rhetoric is more successful than in the last books.

Childhood: Books 1 and 2

Much good must be said of the rhetorical achievement of Book 1. Through rhetoric of character, reinforced by the rhetoric of narration, Book 1 establishes keen practical interest in Maggie and the expectation of a tragic pattern in her life. All the characters except the two Wakems and Stephen are delineated, compared, and contrasted, and Maggie and Tom are firmly placed in relation to each other and to the principal people in their family and town.

In the one conversation that precedes and follows the entrance of Maggie, tossing her hair and dragging her bonnet, we learn that she is at once beautiful, vibrant, and intelligent, and also unconventional, spoiled, and willful, and thus sure to be in conflict with others' expectations of her. What will happen to her as a result becomes the immediate and central question. As Book 1 progresses, her confrontations with relatives illustrate the pattern of alternating rebellion and dangerous dependency, which must lead to disaster unless she can mature. And despite a tone of mild humor in the narration, no miracle of maturation is suggested as probable.

In representing Maggie, the narrator of Book 1 is distinctly present and suitably distanced. By adult syntax and diction, by Biblical and classical metaphors, and by ironic inflations, the narrator detaches herself from Maggie's mind and deflates her exaggerations; the same detachment is obviously expected of the knowledgeable reader. But by many compassionate references to the sorrows of childhood, by direct analysis of Maggie's mixed character and real needs, and by direct expressions of pity, the narrator urges sympathy for the real suffering that is and is to come. Though the use of ''poor Maggie'' is a danger signal, the narrator's attitude is balanced at this point and sets up an expectation of similar poise when Maggie's problems get more complex.

By contrast to the exceptional Maggie, Tom is ''one of those lads that grow everywhere in England (1:45, chap. 5); he draws interest almost wholly from his relationship to her. He is presented with the amused lenience of a benevolent and knowing narrator, who understands and visibly expects the reader to understand that Tom urgently requires assurance of superiority to his more intelligent sister and can get it only by being a boy, a benefactor, and a master. His pleasing and repellent qualities are carefully balanced, so that the latter can never make us forget the former; if an egoism lurks in his every kindness, a streak of sensibility appears after every severity. Thus he captures our interest and concern, making us wonder what he can become, whether anyone will ever rouse and form his latent best qualities, and particularly what effect he will have on his sister's utterly different personality.

Tom's importance to Maggie in the plot is prepared for and stressed by the continual enlargement on their diversity: his realism versus her imagination, his rational foresight and self-approval versus her passionate impulse and self-reproach, his ineptitude for books versus her quickness and relish, and above all, his desire to punish wrongdoers versus her desire to forgive and be forgiven. Since it is soon evident that Maggie will do some serious wrong and that she is slavishly dependent on Tom, it is also clear that their very basic contrasts will make him the principal figure in her almost inevitable tragedy.

Maggie's idolatrous subservience to Tom is the most unpleasing and dangerous feature of her personality. If we are to sympathize with it at all or with her final inability to escape it, we need to understand it quickly and clearly. Much is explained by her isolation in a small circle of relatives who consider her a "mistake of Nature" (1:14, chap. 2); she needs approval and love from a strong and approved other person. The need can best be met by her companion brother, and his personality is domineering but just kindly enough to attract affection.

Yet, even with this explanation, one still feels a lacuna somewhere, a need of some further dramatized, objective basis for this tenacious and nearly uncritical love. It may seem odd to suggest that there is any omission in Book 1, and no one wishes the honesty of the childhood section marred by sentimentality; yet if we are meant to believe that Maggie's adherence to Tom is rooted in a mutual childhood love or that he was more than rarely "good to her," then one or two quarrels (those at Aunt Pullet's and the ensuing run to the gypsies, for instance) should have been excised to make room for more than the "one of their happy mornings" (1:57, chap. 5), which is allotted only two pages. Here a rhetoric of events is needed to explain Maggie's attachment.

The portraits and analyses of Maggie and Tom would not alone establish the pattern of inevitable tragedy for her. Both children are done with too much narrative wit and affection, which suggest that they could outgrow their foibles if given a little wise love and training. The assurance of tragedy is projected through their relatives, who embody the rest of St. Ogg's society, its mores, limited choices, and formative pressures. The representation of these characters is crucial to the distancing of both Maggie and Tom because it tells us to what degree they really are victims and are to be pitied as such.

Even before the two children appear, we hear their probable futures in their parents' conversation. Mr. Tulliver is made sympathetic by his love and defense of Maggie, but he sees no future for her abilities and will do nothing to develop them. He will, in fact, encourage her dependence on himself and Tom; but his son he will mold to a norm as thoroughly and insensitively as Mrs. Tulliver tries to mold Maggie. The mother's trivial norms, peevish nagging, and partiality for Tom create a pitying counter-partiality for the unconventional child. Nevertheless, Maggie's willfulness and passion are most exposed in this relationship: she needs training that her mother cannot give, and she will come to grief for lack of it. Nor can Mrs. Tulliver guide Tom's growth; she encourages the very faults that mark him a true Dodson. These early parental failures will help preserve the reader's sympathy for Maggie as she becomes more dependent on the only loves she finds, and for Tom as he becomes less a loving brother and more a demanding Dodson.

Both Tulliver parents are essentially in proper sympathetic perspective. The Dodson relatives present more of a rhetorical challenge. They are among the principal destructive agents in Maggie's tragedy because they are stronger than her parents and so overbearing that any act of independence must turn into self-destructive rebellion (as in the hair-cutting episode). But the Dodsons are also to have credit as sources of Tom's steadiness and as practical counters to Maggie's erratic disposition. They must

therefore be felt as very oppressive yet credible and as very unsympathetic yet not repulsive. George Eliot tries to achieve the
former effect by lengthy representation and the latter by lacing
the representation with humor.

In general, the detailed representation works well to convey the
oppression, but it does lose some effect from a tendency to
caricature. Mrs. Glegg's rudeness and Mrs. Pullet's irrational
melancholy are narratively exaggerated as Maggie's and her
parents' traits are not, and as these two women seem just a little
less real, so also does the hopelessness of Maggie's situation with
them. This same tendency to caricature allows the Dodsons to
talk and be talked about too much for what they accomplish formally. Inflated dialogue and descriptions slow the movement of
events and cause these minor characters at times to overshadow
the protagonists.

Readers seem to experience an inverse correlation between the
Dodsons' credibility and their humor. If we believe in them, it is
hard to be amused. Rhetorical analysis, however, asks what
degree of humor is proper for their function in a tragedy. They
must not be too funny if we are to think much about their
destructiveness, but some good-natured humor will help us
believe in their virtues and their few kind acts (especially Mrs.
Glegg's). George Eliot gets around the problem by turning her
narrative humor mostly on their harmless bouts with each other.
In describing the Gleggs at home, for instance, she combines her
own highly educated syntax and diction with their ignorant ideas
and colloquial diction, lacing all with a tone of mock-honor that
comically diminishes them:

> Mrs Glegg had both a front and back parlour in her excellent
> house at St. Ogg's, so that she had two points of view from
> which she could observe the weakness of her fellow-beings, and
> reinforce her thankfulness for her own exceptional strength of
> mind. From her front windows she could look down the Tofton
> Road . . . and note the growing tendency to ''gadding about''
> in wives of men not retired from business, together with a prac-
> tice of wearing woven cotton stockings, which opened a dreary

prospect for the coming generation; and from her back win-
dows she could look down the pleasant garden . . . and observe
the folly of Mr Glegg in spending his time among ''them
flowers and vegetables.'' (1:184–85, chap. 12)

This passage, like its total context, is amusing satire; it also effectively prepares later response to Maggie and Tom. For it contains
the stress on appearances, the elevation of household custom into
moral issue, and the total absence of charity and humility that
form the mold into which Tom and Maggie are to be pressed.
Here we truly sympathize with her resistance and regret his
capitulation.

But if we find the Dodsons essentially true and occasionally
funny, we must still question if they are not rendered repulsive
beyond redemption by the narrator's explanations of their
motives. By the end of Book 1 the reader may dislike them
thoroughly,[7] a feeling that will then be increased by their gross
humiliation of the bankrupt Tullivers and be modified only partially by the long narrative explanation of them in Book 4,
chapter 30.

In summary, Book 1 is weighted with an excess of Maggie's
woes and Dodson talk, so that essential plot incidents are too few
for its length. And its humor does diminish somewhat our sense
of a tragedy in preparation. But it does sketch firmly Maggie's
basic traits and those of all the Tullivers and Dodsons who will influence her tragic failure, and it does show how heavily the odds
are against her. At this Book's end, we feel reasonably convinced
that, in a student's colloquialism, Maggie ''hasn't got a
chance.''

Book 2, also long, advances the plot only by the lawsuit and the
introduction of Philip Wakem. This introduction may necessitate
the concentration on Tom's schooling rather than Maggie's;
nevertheless, Philip's rapid rapport with Maggie requires only a
few pages, while the protracted analysis of Tom's academic
misery occupies most of the Book.

Some account of this misery would be needed to maintain sympathy for Tom when the mental and emotional sterility of his education is evidenced in his later behavior. But the record exceeds the rhetorical requirements. We need to know something of everything in Book 2: Philip's basic character, the nature of Tom's education, his inaptitude for it and its unsuitability for him, Maggie's and Philip's similar response to intellectual stimuli, the quality of their friendship from its very inception, and the collisions and cool cordialities of the two boys. Two things we do not need: protracted incident and protracted narrative discussion. Some of Tom's jarring with Philip and the episode of Mr. Poulter and his sword might have been condensed without loss; and the narrator need not explain Tom's situation with so much amplification on Mr. and Mrs. Stelling, the "inferior clergy," or British education "in those distant days." George Eliot admitted to being "beguiled by love of my subject in the first two volumes" (*GEL*, 3:317); she shows it most in the narrator, who depicts and discusses very minor events far beyond their importance in the novel.

While Tom is at King's Lorton, Maggie has a year or so at "Miss Firniss's boarding school," the place that indoctrinates her further in her social duties and to which she will plan to return for refuge from temptation. Now since the barrenness of Maggie's education is so devastating to her, and since she, not Tom, is the true center of the novel, some condensation of his school days was surely in order so as to allot a minimal one or two out of seven chapters to hers. How else shall we give a well-informed and motivated sympathy to her desperate grasp at what seems a wider cultural and emotional life than that of a teacher where she has already been a stunted and unhappy student?

Book 2, then, continues very well the rhetoric of characterization, advancing our comprehension and balanced sympathy for three main persons. But it goes awry in the rhetoric of event and narration by sheer excess of both.

Middle Growth: Books 3 to 5

When the never-really-Golden Gates of childhood have been

passed, the adolescent development of the protagonist and her brother must confirm their personality contrasts and must prepare the reader to accept the inevitability of a final clash and a tragic denouement. All the characters except Stephen Guest have been established, so distancing now depends more heavily on a rhetoric of events that move toward a climax and on a rhetoric of narration that constantly but unoffensively guides and prepares responses.

Establishing distance through events in Books 3 through 5 is complicated by the fact that Maggie and Tom share almost nothing of each other's experiences; their one significant scene together is the confrontation over Philip Wakem in Book 5. Events, therefore, must be so arranged that each remains large in our interest, that their divergences, especially over Philip, prepare for new conflict, and that Tom's hold on Maggie's mind remains credible and sympathetic yet becomes increasingly ominous.

The balancing of interest is accomplished structurally by bringing Maggie and Tom together during the family scenes and interspersing these with one to three chapters at a time on their separate careers. To make this arrangement, George Eliot employs a technique new to her, the deliberate alteration of chronology so that one event will condition our response to another. After Bob Jakin has relieved Maggie's depression by the gift of books, one might expect that the next chapter would cover his assistance to Tom by setting him up in trade. Instead, Maggie's first meeting with Philip in the Red Deeps is placed before the trading venture, although the latter preceded it by a year (2:68, 89, chap. 34).

This placement has several effects: it alternates the record of the young people's struggles, so that neither is absent too long; it mitigates the emotional concentration of the scenes with Philip, which would otherwise have followed for four consecutive chapters; and most of all, it modifies our judgments of both Tom and Maggie. The chapter on Tom's trading, standing just before that in which Maggie succumbs to Philip's persuasions, emphasizes that however pharisaical Tom is about his right deeds, still they *are* right, and he *is* restoring the family happiness and stability, while Maggie decidedly is not.[8] When she too perceives this difference and yields still more to his moral authority, her submission will be more plausible to the reader.

To prepare Tom's final hold on Maggie's conscience, the events of his adolescence must show him still alternating between tenderness and severity but fixating inexorably in the severity, doing right but becoming increasingly self-righteous. The reader must alternate between admiration and regret but always have understanding. Thus he will be prepared to deplore Tom's final behavior but not despise him—or Maggie.

Four main events occur in Tom's life in Books 3 through 5: he enters business, signs the curse on Wakem, stops Maggie's meetings with Philip, and pays Mr. Tulliver's debts. The first is practical, alleviating action, hence sympathetic in itself. The second and third are made tolerable by evidence that they flow, at least partially, from fundamental loyalty to family, a quality that is good in itself and is also the source of Tom's determination to pay the debts. In the attack on Philip, however, Tom's total want of humility, sensitivity, or compassion is so insufferable that one questions whether he is not unjustly manipulated and over-distanced in favor of Philip. But George Eliot keeps him essentially in character, and even in this his ugliest moment, she offers some truth in what Tom says to mitigate our revulsion at the way he says it; Maggie *has* used deceit on her father and brother and Philip *does* speak a deal of "high-flown nonsense" (2:116, 122, chap. 37). We extenuate Tom's conduct, but not without strain. It takes all the power and pathos of the two chapters in which he pays the debts to diminish the distance effected by the scene in the Red Deeps. Like Maggie, we feel at the end of Book 5 that Tom *is* good, despite all; but unlike her, we are not convinced that his faults are redeemed.

Because events create ambivalence, and because no character can fully and fairly evaluate Tom's development during this period, we depend heavily on the rhetoric of narration. In this novel the narrator is able to display omniscience about a badly faulted character without being herself unpleasant, nagging, or obtrusive. She authoritatively names Tom's personal qualities; she explains his thoughts and acts, as he himself could not do; she mediates between him and Maggie to assure justice to him: "Surely there was some tenderness and bravery mingled with the worldliness and self-assertion of that little speech; but Maggie held it as dross, overlooking the grains of gold . . ." (2:39, chap. 32). Most of all the narrator makes sure that we comprehend the mixed motives behind Tom's rise in the world. As he starts out, the narrator says:

> At sixteen, the mind that has the strongest affinity for fact cannot escape illusion and self-flattery; and Tom, in sketching his future, had no other guide in arranging his facts than the suggestions of his own brave self-reliance . . . . he would be like his uncle Deane—get a situation in some great house of business and rise fast. . . . He would provide for his mother and sister, and make every one say that he was a man of high character. (1:353-54, chap. 25)

The mildly amused tone, the references to Tom's real and worthy qualities, and the attribution of his illusion to youth all create a favorable attitude toward his coming efforts. Then when he has succeeded precisely as he anticipated, the reader can both deplore and pity his paradoxical moral failure: his achievements have prepared him to reject his highest obligation, to love and provide for Maggie.

Tom can reject Maggie in the end only because she gives him the opportunity, which means that her adolescent years must confirm her childhood dependence on him. The reader must see and comprehend her ongoing division between becoming her own woman and remaining forever her father's "little wench" and her brother's "little sister."

Until the return of Philip, Maggie's life is externally uneventful. Hence it lies with the narrator to present her solitary inward drama with a sympathy controlled by a wider vision than the girl's own. The narrator steadily pities Maggie; but only after giving internal views of her family members to explain their behavior does she focus on her "sense of loneliness, and utter privation of joy" (2:27, chap. 32). Even then she maintains detachment by distinguishing Maggie's "soul's hunger" from her "illusions of self-flattery" (2:29) and her feeling that she is the "only girl in the civilized world of that day" (2:31) with such troubles.

When Maggie discovers *The Imitation of Christ*, the narrator carefully weighs its values and liabilities for her, the "inmost truth" it offers against her aptitude to misunderstand and respond excessively (2:34-39 passim, chap. 32). This balancing betrays no uncertainty in the narrator. Rather, she knows both Maggie's mind and the wide historical world beyond her, and by well-chosen diction, she relates them and evaluates her response. Thus she draws readers into a bond of sympathy for a mistake such as "we all" make. The diction also points to the deep cause of Maggie's mistake, her dependency on "a brother" and "Teacher" whose words are an "unquestioned message" (2:35-36). When Tom is much absent and when she can no longer endure a Kempis, she will be ready for the authority and message of Philip Wakem, whom she has "continually recalled" as "a brother and teacher" (3:46, chap. 33). This parallel diction prepares the reader for yet another mistake.

The meetings in the Red Deeps are the central events in Maggie's adolescence and will be crucial in her final conflict. Her views and Philip's must therefore be clearly represented, and the narrator's interpretation must be a consistent preparation for whatever response is to be elicited in Book 6. Philip and the narrator speak the same language in negatively judging Maggie's asceticism; his comment on her "resignation" (2:94, chap. 35) echoes the narrator's on her "renunciation" (2:35, chap. 32). But Philip seeks a remedy through deceitful actions, which the narrator—at this point—does not approve. In two long analyses of Philip's reflections on the proposed meetings (2:62-63, chap. 33; 2:99-100, chap. 35), the narrator uncovers the lad's conscious and subconscious motives, grants all extenuating factors, but still clearly indicates his fault in persuading himself and interfering with Maggie's conscience. Maggie's own inner prompting is recorded with diction clearly favoring the "severe monotonous warning'' against loss of ''the simplicity and clearness of her life'' (2:91, chap. 35). When she capitulates, the narrator calls it a ''defeat'' caused by her snatching at Philip's ''sophistry'' (2:97). The single defect in this narrative analysis is that the narrator does not even suggest a large hiatus in Maggie's thinking: perhaps she could not be independent *now* of her father's and brother's wrong feelings, but she never even imagines having such freedom in a future time worth waiting for. This is a major sign of her unwholesome dependence, and we might expect the otherwise all-analyzing narrator to notice it.

Surely we might also expect the narrator's evaluation of the meetings to remain consistent. In Book 5 they are a source of disturbance and deceit; as such, they distance Maggie and especially Philip, their instigator, by a pitying regret, regret for their loneliness and need of mutual sympathy but also for their moral weakness in capitulating. The firmness of judgment in Book 5 will create a problem of distancing when the meetings are reconsidered in Book 6.

Like the meetings themselves, Philip's premature declaration of love is a demand he makes on Maggie because he cannot wait in patience for her possible growth in love or for possible right conditions for fulfillment. In itself this demand distances him as a faulted character who must learn selflessness. In the total rhetoric of events, the declaration is crucial because it displays the essential qualities of their love and so prepares—or should prepare—a firm attitude in both narrator and implied reader regarding their future.

On the one hand, Philip's deformity and especially his morbidity about it produce a mild revulsion, making us anticipate Lucy's later sense of his and Maggie's ''physical incongruity'' (2:225, chap. 46). Yet, despite his sensitivity to his handicap and his extra-refined taste, and despite the narrator's negative, stereotyped comparisons of his nature to a woman's (2:100, chap. 35; 109, chap. 36; 250, chap. 47), it is plain enough that Philip is fully a man who wants and knows that he wants a normal, adult sexual love (chaps. 33, 35, 36 passim). He is not, like Casaubon in *Middlemarch*, looking for an admirer or amanuensis, but for a loving wife. It is hard not to feel that he should have her.

But if Philip is not Casaubon, Maggie is all too much like Dorothea in assuming that the companionship of a teacher can be a substitute for sexual love.[9] Evidence is abundant that she can feel only admiration for Philip's mind, pity for his body, and gratified pride at his affection for and appreciation of her. He offers what she wants from Tom, and she thinks of him as a brother and of her love as self-sacrifice for his happiness. In the Red Deeps, the reader knows clearly enough what to think and hope regarding their marriage, far more clearly than he will know in Book 6.

After Tom has halted the meetings in the Red Deeps, the final two events of Book 5—the payment of the debts and Mr. Tulliver's death—are designed to repair our battered sympathy for Tom, effect his reconciliation with Maggie, and transfer his father's authority wholly to him. Characters and events carry the rhetoric of these chapters. Mr. Tulliver's restored honor pleases, because he is so likable; his death carries no excessive pathos because we have never hoped much for him, only for his children. Their reconciliation is credible because it repeats the familiar pattern, and is pleasing because we still like Tom. But the events are dangerous because Mr. Tulliver's death removes the chief obstacle between Maggie and Philip and increases Tom's control over Maggie without increasing his ability to love her or to respect her freedom of choice. Worse, no events of Books 3 through 5 seem to have increased Maggie's self-knowledge or self-control. She still makes choices impulsively and adheres to them only until her spirit is worn and a stronger personality can overpower her. Thus, as the reader approaches Book 6, he finds his expectation of tragedy and his practical concern for the heroine in a tension demanding resolution.

The Final Crisis: Books 6 and 7

The two final Books are, from the viewpoint of fictional rhetoric, the most troublesome portion of the novel. The new relationships of Maggie, Tom, Philip, and Stephen Guest raise significant problems about the kinds and degrees of sympathy due these characters, their situations, and their decisions.

To begin with, Maggie, in facing the crisis of her passion for Stephen, is finally brought to several real choices about her life, which must lead decisively to her maturity or stunt it irreparably. The reader should have clear means to determine whether her decisions are wise in themselves and whether she has made them freely or not. Only thus can he know how to respond to them—with sympathetic acquiescence, sympathetic regret, delight, relief, pain, or what. And if her choices are to become wise and free at this late date in the novel, some very strong and startling circumstances are required to explain such a change, since every event till now has led us to expect the tragedy of a crushed personality.

Also, if Tom is really the first figure after Maggie, it is necessary that he maintain a credible importance in the events of this part of her life, that the reader be able to comprehend her continuing emotional tie to him despite their infrequent contact. Evidence must be given for any new developments in him that explain his conduct to her, especially his total rejection and presumably total reconciliation.

Philip and Stephen must be adequately represented as they affect Maggie's development and choices, so that the reader may rightly evaluate them as her lovers and possible marriage partners. If they have a relation to Tom that affects his reactions to Maggie, that also must be duly represented.

Finally, given the confusion and moral inadequacies of all the characters, the narrator must function in some way as an interpreter of all and a guide to the responses the author seeks to elicit. Since Maggie in particular is sure to act illogically and passionately, the reader must be enabled to interpret her acts for what they are and thereby pity her tragic destruction for what it really is. It might be argued that narrative guidance is scarcely needed in Books 6 and 7, that we ''have known Maggie a long while, and need to be told, not her characteristics, but her history'' (2:210, chap. 45). But the very explicit presence and instruction of the narrator in the earlier books have created an expectation of continued guidance; any significant narrative withdrawal at this juncture will imply identification with the characters' views and emotions unless some means (diction, dramatic irony, etc.) are used to suggest the realities the characters do not see. (Even in the strictly dramatic mode, Shakespeare found ways to suggest what else Hamlet and Othello might have done and whence came their inevitable and fatal errors.) We must be led somehow to respond to Maggie's history in accordance with its represented facts.

Given these rhetorical requirements, we cannot but note major defects in Books 6 and 7. Various events and character relationships are rhetorically ambiguous or unacceptable in themselves and are made more so by the manner of narration.

The least controversial figure, Philip Wakem, remains an effective foil to Tom in rejecting the family feud and in his abiding love for Maggie and correct understanding of her actions with Stephen. Despite his rivalry, he assesses Stephen accurately enough. Simply as an evaluator of other characters, Philip remains a generally good guide for the reader's judgment and sympathies.

But as a lover, he must act and develop in his own character; and we must know whether his love should be satisfied. At least two puzzling ambiguities cling to the history of Philip as lover.

In Book 5, the narrator was firm in judging the secret meetings in the Red Deeps and the resulting pledge of love: they were unwise, premature, and a source of disturbance. Of course, in a tragic plot, situations change and earlier events may seem better by contrast to later worse ones like the meetings with Stephen. Hence it is psychologically credible that Maggie now views the meetings with Philip as a source of peace and moral security and that Philip clings to their memory even after recognizing his error. But we do not expect a complete reversal of the narrator's prior judgment, which we apparently have. No comments, no touches of irony, no qualifying diction even, are offered to warn us that Maggie's and Philip's views are not fully acceptable, that the meetings are still to be considered as a contributing cause, *not* a nearly effectual preventive of Maggie's tragedy. Indeed, the Conclusion elevates the "mistake" into a sacred event and memory as Philip haunts the Red Deeps, "where the buried joy seemed still to hover—like a revisiting spirit" (2:407), a view with which the narrator seems fully to concur.

A still deeper and unresolved ambivalence is created by Philip's hopeless love. Presumably, we should feel about this much as we do about Adam Bede's love for Hetty—we should sympathize with it but desire that it not be satisfied. The love scene in Book 5 and Maggie's confidences to Lucy (chap. 42) prove that her feeling for Philip is not and never can be a woman's love for her lifetime sexual partner. Her refusal even to ask Tom's consent is clearly motivated less by subservience to him than by desire to postpone or escape an unwanted marriage.

Obviously, for Philip's happiness as much as Maggie's, we cannot wish her to marry him under such a condition. Presumably the knowing narrator does not wish us to wish it. Or does she? Are we not left with a confused sense that Maggie *is* somehow bound in honor to Philip, that he *was* "given to her that she might make his lot less hard" (2:334, chap. 53), and that she would be wrong to forsake him? This confusion stems largely from the inadequate distancing of the narrator's mind from Maggie's throughout these two Books—a problem that will be discussed later.

But ambivalence also arises from the portrayal of Philip's own love. Here we should understand, even share, his strong feeling for Maggie, but not share his desire for the marriage. We should regret Philip's pain, while realizing that he made it worse by his premature demands and rejoicing that at least it is teaching him a new selflessness and sympathy. But Maggie is so genuinely lovable and Philip's need is so great that sympathy for his love is urged too strongly. We want it to be satisfied. Each scene contributes to this effect, but none more emphatically than Chapter 47, in which Philip wins his father's consent. The dialogue structure of the scene automatically allies us with Philip. And his strength of purpose, coolness, and self-control in this risky situation, in spite of his high-strung nature, convince us more firmly than ever of the force of his love for Maggie and win such respect and sympathy for him that we cannot wish his disappointment. Even the ''new light'' on Wakem, yielding his irascibility and pride to secure his son's happiness, adds strength to the effect. One wonders if this scene, like Hetty Sorrel's journey, should not have been omitted or modified.

The ambiguity about Philip's love is not resolved by his final letter. Taken alone, it allows two readings: (1) despite its overblown diction and syntax, it proves that Philip has learned genuine selflessness through suffering; in this case, the letter partially reconciles us to his fate, yet also increases our pity and desire for his happiness; (2) its rhetoric betrays Philip's unhealthy sense of martyrdom—''see how nobly I have suffered''; in that case we still pity him but wish his disappointment to continue teaching him better. And the letter has to be taken alone, for no narrative guidance at all is offered—only the very unreliable rhetoric of Maggie's sobbing penitence and gratitude.

The only subsequent mention of Philip is in the Conclusion. There, contrary to his assertion in his letter that he has entered an ''enlarged life which grows and grows by appropriating the life of others'' (2:372, chap. 56), we are told that he lived out his life ''always solitary,'' that his ''great companionship'' is with the trees of the Red Deeps. Again the absence of any negative interpretation suggests that this is a noble and acceptable resolution of Philip's love. But the reader may not be convinced.

Maggie's second suitor, Stephen Guest, has roused immense critical wrangling about his fitness as an object for her love. Certainly our response to Maggie's most crucial decision is influenced by our response to Stephen himself. For rhetorical purposes he must have only those qualities needed to make her passion and struggle credible in her new circumstances. She has ''just come away from a third-rate schoolroom'' (2:183, chap. 42), aware that she has contracted a ''bad habit of being unhappy'' (2:165, chap. 41) and recoiling from the remembrance of ''the time when she had courted privation'' (2:183, chap. 42). In short, she is ripe for another grasp at love and happiness. To attract her initially,

Stephen need only have a strong, attractive masculinity and sufficient knowledge to converse intelligently on topics outside the usual range offered a provincial governess.[10] But to convince us of her enormous moral conflict and the temporary suspension of her compulsive sense of duty, his portrait would require some depth and detail.

Aside from the distancing notation of "diamond ring, attar of roses, and air of nonchalant leisure" (2:149, chap. 40), only one physical description of Stephen is provided: "a rather striking young man of five-and-twenty, with a square forehead, short dark brown hair standing erect, with a slight wave at the end, like a thick crop of corn, and a half-ardent, half-sarcastic glance from under his well-marked horizontal eyebrows" (2:150-51). This is hardly a sharp visualization of his face or physique. Other references are of the briefest kind, though relatively frequent. All in all, there simply is not enough physical presentation of Stephen to make us feel the force of Maggie's attraction and his functional contrast to Philip. We end up assuming that he must be compellingly handsome because Maggie is attracted so strongly, not because we are able to see with her eyes.

The evidence for Stephen's mental and moral powers must be carefully weighed. His opening actions and conversations are most trivial and betray his demeaning view of women (chap. 40); the dry narrative irony is plainly a negative comment. And throughout Book 6, Stephen's better qualities are overshadowed by disproportionate representation of his vanity. Nevertheless, he has finer facets that emerge *in Maggie's presence* and that appeal to her. He has done serious reading and is capable of serious discussion. He discerns and reverences the genuine spirituality of Dr. Kenn; he is also aware of his own defects and is capable of a certain irony at his own expense (chaps. 41, 45, 46, passim). He is attracted by Maggie's perception of his defects and boldness in railing him, qualities he has not expected in women. And when he is mastered by passion for a new kind of woman, he is perfectly prepared to marry her without consideration of caste snobbery. Stephen is neither a fop nor a rake, and Maggie knows he is not.

We may not despise him, nor her for loving him. But we must still question whether Stephen's moral traits are urged strongly enough to explain their outweighing Maggie's moral compulsions. The presentation of his vanity leaves a strong smell of attar of roses, which we may feel that Maggie should have sensed.

Stephen, then, may be fit to satisfy Maggie's immediate cravings, but he is hardly fit to be her lifetime partner. The initial portrait probably convinces a reader of that. But once Stephen becomes serious about Maggie, only Philip's voice attests to his inferior nature. All other characters think him a great prize for any woman, and the narrator is oddly silent. The caustic diction marking his first appearance nearly disappears, and the developing love is portrayed nonjudgmentally, with a good measure of sympathy for both lovers and with full representation of all their emotions and rationalizations. A narrator who can see and depict so much presumably could evaluate Stephen. If he is unworthy of Maggie, we might expect some clear implication that a marriage would be regrettable for *that* reason, but all the stress is laid on the uncertain "duty" of renunciation because of the two almost-engagements. We might also expect a suggestion that Stephen, like Philip, evokes a tendency in Maggie's character to choose an unsatisfactory mate and orient herself toward an unfulfilling marriage—the only kind she has ever seen. Without that suggestion, it seems that if she could ever meet a Stephen who was not duty-bound, she might be made happy. Her tragedy then becomes a result of chance, not of her background and character.

When Maggie turns away from Stephen, she deliberately returns to Tom. Though these two acts are linked in her psyche, the first does not necessarily require the second. If we are to sympathize with Maggie's impulse to return to Tom, if we are to tolerate his rejection, still hope for another reconciliation, and respond sympathetically when it occurs, then we need first to find a justification in Tom himself. We need to know all that can explain his conduct in Books 6 and 7 and all that will explain whether and why the reconciliation is a true and permanent change in his character and relationship with Maggie.

Tom's severity to all Maggie's past errors largely explains his act of rejection, but he is, after all, no more a self-righteous Dodson than his Aunt Glegg, and he also has his father's injunction and example to obey. And Maggie is ready to submit to the moral guidance and correction which he has always been only too ready to supply. His persistent refusal to shelter or uphold her requires some rhetoric of events to assure us that he *cannot*, that something has happened to him in Book 6 that will explain, if not justify, his act in Book 7.

Tom is visible too little in Book 6 for this book to explain much; and here, I think, not in the development of the Maggie-Stephen story, is rooted that "want of proportionate fullness" in the last third of the novel (*GEL*, 3:317).[11] Yet two things have happened to Tom, one seen but little, the other merely hinted at.

We are notified in Book 6 of Tom's continuing success, climaxed by his return to the Mill. This event furthers his character development by aggravating his pride. But it also generates a certain sympathy for him like that felt in Book 5 when he paid the debts. We do feel a satisfaction for his sake and a sympathy for the disappointment Maggie will cause him. These effects are limited, however, by the fact that Tom appears only in three of fourteen chapters in Book 6. And the little we see is a rather repelling young man whose monomaniacal concentration on work has destroyed his zest for its rewards.

Except perhaps one reward. According to Bob Jakin, Tom has developed "a soft place in him. It was about a little black spaniel . . .he made a fuss to get. But since then, summat's come over him . . . (2:192-93, chap. 43). The spaniel, of course, is Lucy's and the "summat" is therefore disappointed love. Now if there is anything we need to see in Tom Tulliver, it is a soft place, a vibration of "tender fibres" beyond his control. Except at his father's death, we have not seen those since his childhood; and we need something to support Maggie's continuing faith in them.

Bob's remark is not the only thread of this complication left dangling. Earlier the narrator has told us:

> since his education at Mr. Stelling's, . . . he had often thought
> that when he got older he would . . . show himself equal to any
> of his contemporaries at St. Ogg's, who might consider
> themselves a grade above him in society, because their
> fathers . . . had large oil mills. (1:297, chap. 20)

In Book 6 we learn that Stephen Guest is heir to St. Ogg's largest
oil-mill. Surely something significant for our responses could
have been made of this competition for love and status between
Stephen and Tom—one man whose soft life makes soft behavior
easy, another whose capacity for tenderness has been attenuated
by suffering and incessant labor. Tom never meets Stephen in the
book, and he has only one indirectly recorded adult conversation
with Lucy (2:297-98, chap. 51). Yet how much might have been
done rhetorically by presenting a conflict in Tom's mind caused
by Stephen's ascendancy, Maggie's injury to Lucy and disgrace of
the family, and the chance of Maggie's taking Stephen and thus
freeing Lucy. However rigid his character, Tom is not incapable
of mixed emotional response, and development of his love-event
would have balanced the first and last sections of the book and
carried out neatly his parallelism to Maggie. It would also have
gone far to motivate his commercial endeavors and to explain the
virulence of his rejection of Maggie, Lucy's "betrayer."

With the rhetoric of events undeveloped, we look to characters
to guide our response to Tom in these last Books, but they are little more help than with Maggie. No one objectively judges his actions. Maggie is too conscious of her own guilt to measure the
justice of his punishment. Mrs. Glegg reprobates his unjust
response but does not understand it. Almost everyone else in St.
Ogg's approves it. No one can guide us to comprehension or appropriate distance but the narrator.

She succeeds rather well in dealing with Tom in this event. She
prepares for his initial cruelty by a reminder that the "old
respectability" has just been restored through his "steady self-
government" and by a description of his current expectation of
disgrace. She refrains from any condemnatory comment and offers only a burst of admiration for Mrs. Tulliver's "draught of

simple human pity'' (2:343, chap. 54). The real obstacle to our sympathy with Tom is not this spontaneous first rejection of Maggie, but his persistence even after Stephen's letter. Here, as before, the narrator explains Tom's worst moments:

> Poor Tom! he judged by what he had been able to see; and the judgment was painful enough to himself. He thought he had the demonstration of facts observed through the years by his own eyes which gave no warning of their imperfection, that Maggie's nature was utterly untrustworthy . . . he would act on that demonstration at any cost; but the thought of it made his days bitter to him. Tom, like every one of us, was imprisoned within the limits of his own nature . . . if you are inclined to be severe on his severity, remember that the responsibility of tolerance lies with those who have the wider vision. (2:366, chap. 56)

This effective passage wins compassionate tolerance for Tom in several ways. It directly expresses pity; it stresses his faulty vision, which he cannot know of or help, and his own suffering from it. By the word *imprisoned* it exonerates him from the full responsibility of a free man; by the phrase *like every one of us* it joins Tom, narrator, and mock-reader within similar limits. And it implies that the reader's responsibility, if indeed he has wider vision, is to tolerate Tom as much as Maggie.

But if Tom's vision is so faulty and his following it so determined, is he capable of that final ''revelation to his spirit, of the depth in life, that had lain beyond his vision (2:399, chap. 58)? Yet another reconciliation is credible, since the crisis precipitating it is as severe as the quarrel. And doubtless an accurate representation would show the event to be highly emotional But could Tom really recognize the depth of Maggie's love or his own lack and thus achieve a permanent reconciliation? The narrator tries to convince us by intensity of diction:

> the full meaning . . . rushed upon his mind . . . with so over- powering a force . . . that he was unable to ask a question . . . . Tom [sat] pale with a certain awe and humiliation . . . . a mist

> gathered over the blue-grey eyes, and the lips found a word they could utter: the old childish—"Magsie!" (2:399)

The implication is that an inner experience so complete and so devastating to Tom's usual defenses must really alter his character—tragically, ironically too late.[12] But that is an interpretation that flows only from the diction and is unsupported by any previous representations of either Tom or Maggie. Are we to suppose that, had they survived the flood, Maggie would have made no more errors or Tom would never again have reproached her? The rhetoric of diction may temporarily beguile us, but it jars with both events and characters as we have known them, and we surrender to it only because we know that this event is The End.

We have seen that the rhetoric affecting Philip, Stephen, and Tom as objects for Maggie's crucial decisions is sometimes inappropriate, ambiguous, or unconvincing in Books 6 and 7. We may now ask if the rhetoric surrounding Maggie herself as decision-maker succeeds in explaining her acts and distancing her as the protagonist of a psychological tragedy of wasted potential. All the expectations that have been building from the earliest pages have prepared for this kind of tragedy; hardly any evidence could suffice at this point to turn Maggie into a spiritually educated or fulfilled and gloriously heroic woman or martyr. We have a right, then, to expect that the rhetoric will indicate two things; what saving options Maggie would really have if she were not too psychically battered to choose them, and the fact that she *is* psychically destroyed, not gloriously redeemed.

Obviously, Maggie's crucial decision is her renunciation of Stephen Guest. How shall we respond to that? What does George Eliot, through her created events and characters and her "second self," suggest is Maggie's best option, and how does she interpret the quality of her decision?

All forms of rhetoric concur that Maggie is either struggling or drifting and never really decisive in her early relationship with Stephen, and that her going alone with him in the boat is a grave indiscretion. But that act, once done, does alter the implications of all future acts; and the opinions of the characters are so varied that clear and convincing narrative rhetoric is most needful if we are to be glad of Maggie's final renunciation or compassionately to regret it, or to see either option as tragic for her.

The rhetoric of events is of little help. Stephen is correct that their ''elopement,'' once begun, must end either in marriage or in disgrace, that no further possibility exists of mercifully sparing Lucy and Philip (2:330-33, chap. 53). But Maggie is correct that her happiness in marriage would spring from their misery. The ''world'' would accept Mrs. Guest, but she would never accept herself. It will not accept a repentant Miss Tulliver, and she will not accept shelter with her Aunt Glegg. Events therefore present a dilemma but guide us to no sense of a best possible—or least dreadful—solution.

The characters are even more confusing guides. Tom and the ''world's wife'' would have borne a marriage concurrent with the elopement, but do not want it later. Lucy still has love and hopes and therefore desires the renunciation she admires. Philip has no hopes but retains his judgment of Stephen, and Maggie herself never doubts that marrying Stephen would be a ''contradiction with her past self in her moments of strength and clearness'' (2:390, chap. 58). Thus everyone except Stephen and Dr. Kenn assumes that Maggie's refusal is and ought to be permanent. Stephen is hardly disinterested, and Dr. Kenn, though ''powerfully'' inclined to think an ''ultimate marriage'' is the ''least evil,'' is uncertain of what is best and apparently remains so.

Where, then, is the narrator's opinion to be found? Nowhere clearly enough to unite the critics, that is certain. One critic believes that the narrator's view is Dr. Kenn's, another that it is Philip's, most critics, that it is the same as Maggie's.[13] It is clear that the narrator does not sanction a precipitate cleavage of ties and agrees with Dr. Kenn that Maggie's return was right. Yet she never hints at any ethical, psychologically maturing alternatives beyond the return. That Maggie cannot think logically enough to choose an alternative is her inescapable tragedy. But if we are to feel that tragedy pityingly, we should know what other course could have saved her. None is suggested. We assume that the narrator approves Maggie's ultimate decision, not because she clearly implies so, but because she preponderantly uses the girl's viewpoint. The reader is virtually sealed into Maggie's agonized, confused mind; small wonder that he is also confused. He may decide what he does think, but may never be sure what George Eliot meant him to think.

Rejection of Stephen does not, as has been noted, force Maggie into a choice of Tom. She goes to her brother not just because he is her only immediate alternative shelter, but because she is so ridden with guilt and grief that she craves his reproaches as the voice of her own conscience, as a necessary help to her better purpose (2:340, chap. 54). This may be masochism and immaturity, but the narrator does not detach herself from Maggie's view to qualify it. She again relies on Dr. Kenn, who asserts that Maggie's choice of her "nearest friends" was a "true prompting" sanctioned by the highest Christian principle. But Dr. Kenn can judge only by that principle; he cannot tell us the quality of Tom's character or of Maggie's dependence on him.

Still, on his word, we assume that Maggie is right to return to Tom, who ought to shield and help her. When he doesn't, should she stay in St. Ogg's? She soon learns that staying cannot alleviate her loneliness or provide her livelihood, yet she will not leave till Kenn makes her. The events thus suggest that she is still unfree of St. Ogg's inner control over her psyche, still looking for a life of love to be given her, especially by Tom. Yet again the narrator withholds all comment, irony, or suggestive diction, leaving us only the pathetic diction of Maggie's own viewpoint: "She must be a lonely wanderer. . . rouse herself to receive new impressions—and she was so unspeakably, sickeningly weary! There was no home, no help for the erring . . . . But ought she to complain? Ought she to shrink. . . from the long penance of life . . . ?" (2:387, chap. 58).

Nothing is done narratively to suggest that a new home and fresh impressions are precisely what she needs to give new opportunity and vigor to a life that, at nineteen, should not be finished and despaired of, or that a move, if only Maggie were capable of choice, would be a decisive step toward maturity. Rather, the implication of the total passage is not that she is acting under compulsion and guilt, is tragically damaged, but that she is heroic in her admission of error and disclaimer of personal happiness and is right in her persistent wish to remain in her uncongenial, repressive home society.

The lack of narrative guidance about the quality of Maggie's options and decisions does not seem easily defensible. It is true that the rhetoric of tragedy builds toward ever more intense and painful involvement of the reader with the protagonist, and that we do not want interference between us and Maggie's agony as it comes to a climax. But since her particular tragedy is one of unfulfillment and not of final ennoblement, some technique should create the minimum essential distance that will prevent our adopting Maggie's own distorted views. But in Books 6 and 7, the narrator submerges herself in Maggie's viewpoint,[14] which suggests that George Eliot wants to annihilate all distance between character, narrator, and reader. That hardly seems appropriate—at least, not for the story George Eliot did write about the heroine she actually represented.

Probably the problem could have been solved best, not by returning to the talkative narrator of Books 1 through 5, but by infusing the use of Maggie's viewpoint with such diction as would create dramatic irony, an effect very appropriate and usual to tragedy. Irony, of course, has to be distinguishable as such, and in Books 6 and 7 it seldom is. The best suggestions of distancing diction are ambiguous. Consider a typical passage from Book 7:

> The idea of ever recovering happiness never glimmered in her mind for a moment; it seemed as if every sensitive fibre in her were too entirely preoccupied by pain ever to vibrate again to another influence. Life stretched before her as one act of penitence, and all she craved, as she dwelt on her future lot, was something to guarantee her from more falling: her own weakness haunted her like a vision of hideous possibilities, that

> made no peace conceivable except such as lay in the sense of a
> sure refuge. (2:354, chap. 55)

The mention of the ''idea'' that never occurred to Maggie tells
that it has at least occurred to the narrator, that perhaps the
future does not ''seem'' to her as it does to Maggie. But that
sentence is our only hint of a wider perspective than Maggie's,
drawn from longer experience of human suffering and recovery,
our only hint that the ''hideous possibilities'' are real only
because Maggie's personality is bruised beyond healing. The
passage can just as easily be interpreted as the narrator's moral
approval of Maggie's spirit of penitence and craving for refuge, as
if perpetual guilt and self-punishment and insecurity were to be
honored as virtues.

Nearly all the rhetorical problems of Books 6 and 7 are linked
to this merging of the narrator's view with Maggie's. By it
George Eliot forfeited in the last of her novel the precision of
distance that alone could make a reader accurately comprehend
and appropriately sympathize with her heroine. She also changed
her narrator's personality, making her seem less perceptive and
judicious than before. The problem is not only that wise interpretation is missing, but that the implied interpretation violates
both character and narrator.

But nothing more totally violates our tragic expectations for
Maggie than the novel's final event. When Maggie has burned
Stephen's final letter and uttered her ''cry of self-despair''
(2:391, chap. 58), no other ending is possible for her except to
leave St. Ogg's for some other town where, being what she now
is, she will either fall into more passionate and erratic behavior or
be finally crushed into a spiritless, unhappy conformity (her condition on her arrival at Deanes's). Internally trapped she is, and
end she must, but not by physical death. This is a psychological
tragedy that could have ended credibly only on a coach bound for
some provincial school or home. Instead, Maggie's cry brings in a
flood, so pat upon its cue that the rhetorical effect is almost comic,
is certainly a distressing sense of authorial escapism. This is not
the culmination of a tragedy but an evasion through blissful death

of the consequences of a whole chain of events that have ruined a personality.

And, at this last minute, an attempt is also made to evade the fact of that ruin. In Maggie's final confrontation with the flood, the rhetoric is clearly designed to glorify her as a willing martyr who risks and loses her life to save others. All the diction suggests unparalleled courage, strength, and love inspiring superhuman efforts made under divine protection. Maggie does, of course, have immense emotional powers to activate her in a crisis. What is not convincing is the implication of conscious heroism on her part. Maggie is borne out upon the water without full action of her will, and her eventual fuller consciousness and direction of the boat toward Tom's rescue is largely an act of spontaneous emotion (2:392-95, chap. 58). She has not suddenly become a healed, self-directing woman; she does not decide to rescue her undeserving brother at the cost of her own life, and it is useless for George Eliot to try to glorify her through Tom's amazement or misty eyes. Maggie does not finally choose her life; it is given to her—and taken away in a drowning as fortuitous as the flood itself.[15]

The drowning is clearly designed to be the ultimate rhetoric reconciling the reader to both Tom and Maggie in another kind of fictional ''embrace never to be parted'' (2:400). But neither death is required by either their characters or the preceding events.[16] And we are not reconciled to the contrivance by diction of the ''supreme moment'' or the ''days when they clasped their little hands in love, and roamed the daisied fields together'' (2:400). No prior representation of such perfect and untroubled love supports this vision of love restored.

The drowning ultimately prevents any resolution of the tension between pattern and practical concern for Maggie. Her acts and decisions have followed the pattern of her personality but are not the real cause of her death. Realistically, she could have rescued Tom, been reconciled, and have survived; would she then have lived happily or unhappily with him at the Mill, eventually have married someone new, had another crisis, or what? Drowning by accident is not a tragic destruction in any case; in this case it is actually a rescue from the future. Once the flood starts, there is no imaginable way to end this novel that would really complete its tragic pattern.

This analysis of Books 6 and 7 may seem excessively severe, given the experience of generations of readers who have responded to them with absorbed interest and feeling. This reader does not deny either a like response or the power and beauty of characterization and style in these books. Nevertheless, it must be said that the rhetoric that rouses interest and feeling does not equally meet the demands of intelligent judgment. The extraordinary mimesis is not linked to a coherent interpretation. For that interpretation, the rhetoric of events, character, and overall structure were inadequate in these books; only the narrator could have compensated. And she did not.

Yet if we compare *The Mill* to its predecessor, it can be said that this evasion by the narrator is the lamentable excess of a virtue. One of the principal advances of *The Mill on the Floss* over *Adam Bede* is the narrator's self-effacement in favor of the characters and of reliance on the reader's good sense. Explanations and analyses are hardly ever extraneous or insulting. The characteristic flaw of the narrator of *The Mill* is not, as in *Adam Bede*, a fluctuating, antagonistic, or unwarranted relation to the reader, or a jerking about of his sympathetic distance from the characters, but rather a kind of uneasy confusion about who in the novel is really sympathetic, when, why, and to what degree.

This fumbling guidance occurs chiefly when the narrator is absorbed in the dilemmas of the beloved heroine, when she is torn between the impulse to recognize Maggie's tragic failure as a person and the counter-impulse to glorify her as superior to all others not only in her potential but in her final development. When Maggie's story clearly ''means'' that a gifted and emotional Victorian girl is liable to be so repressed by her society that she becomes even self-defeating, then the represented facts and the theme cohere. But when the rhetoric tries to make the story mean that this repressed girl is to be honored for her compulsions as if she had achieved willing self-conquest and self-fulfillment, then that rhetoric cannot be convincing.

But George Eliot's unsteadiness in interpreting the intricacies of choice implies no corresponding weakness in depicting them. In this area her power has greatly increased. With superb assurance she leads us down the labyrinthine ways of each personality, pointing out traits that we might overlook or that the characters themselves do not recognize. The mental activity of the characters in this novel becomes fully engrossing, far more so than the rather pedestrian external events. This is true not only of Maggie's inner strife; even narrower minds like Stephen's and Tom's create a desire for that further development and analysis which we feel they could sustain. Our sympathy with them is tried by displeasure but never by boredom.

In his journal, George Henry Lewes recorded a doubt whether *The Mill on the Floss* was as interesting as *Adam Bede*: "Neither the story nor the characters take so profound a hold of the sympathies" (*GEL*, 3:292). George Eliot's own critique is more accurate: *The Mill* has "more thought and a profounder veracity" than *Adam Bede*, but *Adam* is "more complete, and better balanced" (*GEL*, 3:374). The increased psychological veracity of the characters in *The Mill on the Floss* is just what does make them seize strongly on our sympathies; if the story does not equally grip us, that is due to the lack of balance, especially of Tom and Maggie in the first and last thirds, and to the dropping or fortuitous completion of some issues and story lines. George Eliot's development as an artist was to be marked by increasing ability both to delineate and to interpret complex people in intricate moral situations.

Notes

1. E. S. Dallas, *The Times*, 19 May 1860, reprinted in *A Century of George Eliot Criticism*, ed. Gordon S. Haight (Boston: Houghton Mifflin Company, 1965), p. 11.
2. George Eliot, *The Mill on the Floss*, Standard Edition in 2 vols. (Edinburgh: William Blackwood and Sons, 189-?), 2:5, chap. 30. This and future citations within the text refer first to volume and page number in this edition. This novel, like all George Eliot's, is divided into Books; but in this one only, she did not number the chapters consecutively

from Book to Book. Most modern editors of reprints have done this for her. For users of these reprints and also to avoid confusion of excess numbers, I have omitted Book numbers and given the consecutively numbered chapter numbers after the references to the Standard Edition.

3. Bernard J. Paris, ''The Inner Conflicts of Maggie Tulliver: A Horneyan Analysis,'' *The Centennial Review* 13 (1969): 166-99, offers a reading of Maggie's psychology that has influenced my view of the novel's formal center and of the kinds and degrees of sympathy due to Maggie and others. His essay is reprinted in *A Psychological Approach to Fiction*, chap. 5.

Some readers of my manuscript questioned what seems a rather loose employment of the term *tragedy*, both here and in the discussion of *Middlemarch* in chap. 4. Yet I think my use of the term conforms to the understanding Eliot and other Victorian novelists had of what they were writing—an action neither so exactly structured as classical tragedy nor requiring so total a destruction of so heroic a protagonist, but nevertheless an action culminating in a disaster of great finality, affecting a person of high potential and destroying his or her ultimate hope of happiness or success. The finality and magnitude of effect make the plot more than ''serious,'' and our concern for the characters involved makes our response more ''pity and terror'' than mere regret or resignation. *Adam Bede* I would call a ''serious plot''; *The Mill on the Floss* and *Middlemarch* (with one qualification) seem to me the Victorian type of tragedy.

I wrote my explication of *The Mill* as tragedy before reading either Jeanette King's *Tragedy in the Victorian Novel* (Cambridge: Cambridge University Press, 1978) or Felicia Bonaparte's *Will and Destiny: Morality and Tragedy in George Eliot's Novels* (New York: New York University Press, 1975). Both view *The Mill* as tragedy, though for different reasons from mine (King, pp. 78-84; Bonaparte, pp. 62-70 and 203-10). Psychological destruction still seems to me the best way to explain the tragedy of Maggie Tulliver.

4. This is one of the titles with which George Eliot experimented. Lewes rejected it as sounding like a child's story, but George Eliot's instinct was good. This title suggests the true focus and plot better than any, including the one finally chosen at Blackwood's suggestion. *GEL*, 3:240, 244.

5. The above was written before I had read either William Buckler's statements that Maggie is ''unchallenged as the protagonist'' and that Tom plays a role second only to hers (''Memory, Morality and Tragic Vision in the Early Novels of George Eliot,'' in *The English Novel in the Nineteenth Century*, ed. George Goodin [Urbana: University of Illinois Press, 1972], pp. 150-52) or John Hagan's analysis of the central subject as the ''nature of Maggie's relation to Tom . . . and the tragic effects of this relation on her life'' (''A Reinterpretation of *The Mill on the Floss*,'' *PMLA* 87 [1972]: 57). Obviously, I agree with Buckler, and I disagree with Hagan only in that I think society and Maggie's own psyche are more responsible for her ruin than he allows.

6. George Levine, ''Intelligence as Deception: *The Mill on the Floss*,'' *PMLA* 80 (1965): 402-9; Bernard Paris, *Experiments in Life: George Eliot's Quest for Values* (Detroit, Mich.: Wayne State University Press, 1965), pp. 156-68; Reva Stump, *Movement and Vision in George Eliot's Novels* (Seattle: University of Washington Press, 1959), pp. 110-34. All offer positive readings of Maggie's moral development; Paris, however, has since altered his view of Maggie, though not his view of George Eliot's view (see *A Psychological Approach to Fiction*, chap. 5).

7. Most early reviewers did dislike them, contrary to the intent of the author, who was "aghast to find them ticketed with such very ugly adjectives" (*GEL*, 3:299).

8. George Eliot gains much the same effect by the placement of chaps. 44 and 51, dealing with Tom's regaining the Mill, each just before one of Maggie's capitulations to Stephen.

9. This comparison has also been noted by Joan Bennett, *George Eliot: Her Mind and Her Art* (Cambridge: University Press, 1954), p. 119.

10. Buckler, p. 158, and Bennett, p. 119, discuss helpfully Stephen's character in relation to Maggie's and his potential for positive change.

11. Barbara Hardy, *The Novels of George Eliot* (London: University of London, The Athlone Press, 1959), pp. 56-57, demonstrates cogently that a delineation of Maggie's passion for Stephen required rapid narration and would have been damaged by much detail. She does not, however, discuss the small role of Tom in these Books.

12. The Macmillan's reviewer questioned "whether if they had not died . . . Tom would not have remained the same Tom, hard and narrow-minded, though the least ray of love and happiness cast over his gloomy life, might have softened and made a thoroughly good man of him" (April 1861, reprinted in *George Eliot and Her Readers*, ed. John Holstrom and Laurence Lerner [New York: Barnes and Noble, 1966], p. 40). I would question not only the fact of any permanent alteration, but whether even love and happiness would have softened him. Had Tom married Lucy Deane, it is hard to imagine that he would have been any other than the Tom of Books 1 and 2, likable and tactless, good-natured and officiously quarrelsome by turns, treating all men as he there treats Philip and Bob Jakin.

13. Bennett, p. 127; Hardy, pp. 54-55; Elizabeth Drew, *The Novel: A Modern Guide to Fifteen English Masterpieces* (New York: Dell Publishing Co., 1963), p. 138; F. R. Leavis, *The Great Tradition* (New York: New York University Press, 1963), p. 44; Leslie Stephen, *George Eliot* (London: Macmillan and Co., 1926), pp. 103-4; and numerous others.

14. Helpful insights on the changed use of viewpoint in Books 6 and 7 are offered by Jerome Thale, *The Novels of George Eliot* (New York: Columbia University Press, 1959), pp. 54-56, and by Milton Reigelman, "Narrative Technique in George Eliot's *The Mill on the Floss*," *Kentucky Philological Association Bulletin* 3 (1976): 7-13.

15. The cause of the drowning is even a physical impossibility. In "The Ending of *The Mill on the Floss*," *Notes and Queries* 11 (1964): 226, Keith Brown pointed out that in a current, water carries all objects at the same speed, hence the fatal machinery would not have overtaken the boat.

16. Among the many critics discussing this issue, the following offer good analyses: U. C. Knoepflmacher, *George Eliot's Early Novels: The Limits of Realism* (Berkeley: University of California Press, 1968), p. 220; Barbara Hardy, "The Mill on the Floss," in *Critical Essays on George Eliot*, ed. B. Hardy (London: Routledge and Kegan Paul, 1970), pp. 46-49; Peter K. Garrett, *Scene and Symbol from George Eliot to James Joyce: Studies in Changing Fictional Mode* (New Haven, Conn.: Yale University Press, 1969), p. 45; and Hagan, "A Reinterpretation," p. 62.

[4]

Felix Holt the Radical

In a comparative and selective study of George Eliot's novels there is a temptation to leap from *The Mill on the Floss* to *Middlemarch* without touching those works of very middling repute that mark her central creative period. But in the eleven years between her best-known novels, George Eliot produced three others that greatly help to explain the advance in every distancing technique to be found in *Middlemarch*. The most representative and therefore most useful for study is *Felix Holt the Radical*.

Silas Marner establishes distance with nearly perfect finesse, but its rhetorical manner is conditioned by its esentially nonrealistic mode. Despite the Dutch-painting fidelity of some descriptions and the rural dialogue, I take the novel to be an apologue of man separated both by betrayal and by choice from his own moral and social nature, but restored by choice of a significant and responsible human relationship. Man is represented by Silas, secondarily by Godfrey Cass; both find restoration in the paternity of Eppie, Silas wholly, Godfrey too little because too late.

Many signs of apologue mark this small classic and create the distance appropriate to its type.[1] Attention is dispersed among Silas, the Cass family, and the folk of Raveloe, and even Silas and Godfrey are two-dimensional; they change in situation more than in profound inner character. Dialogue is minimal, especially from Silas, and the narrator alone presents and overtly explicates most of the story, in a frankly but never offensively didactic manner.

The story occurs "in districts far away" and in "that far-off time" of spinning wheels and superstition, when coincidences scarcely surprise the folk either in or out of a novel, and when the latter can accept them in the glow of legend and moral meaning. Time passes in great leaps, so that the slow accretions of character change cannot occupy the reader's interest, only the meaning of the change completed. All these distancing factors certify the novel as apologue and perfect it as such; they also relieved George Eliot of the rhetorical problems inherent in her usual realistic mode and place this novel partly to the side of her high road of development as artist of sympathy.

With *Romola* she tried to return to the mode of realistic action in a new, non-English setting, and the very factors that graced *Silas Marner* made the Florentine novel a dismal and universally admitted failure. Its guide-book descriptions of Florence, the explicitly Victorian narrative voice, the heavy preponderance of narration over dramatized scene, the stilted rhetoric of its dialogue, and the typed characters, so much explained and so little vivified—all testify that George Eliot's creativity could not bridge the distance between her own nineteenth-century rationalist mentality and the much researched but imaginatively still unfamiliar world of Medicean Florence. The novel's worth and interest lie, not in itself, but only in the history of George Eliot as a writer, and any full-scale discussion of its formal rhetoric would be merely an elaboration of the defects just listed.

But with *Felix Holt* she returned to provincial England of the 1830s and to the problem of the individual's search for a meaningful life in that society. These basic similarities in setting and situation to *The Mill on the Floss* and *Middlemarch* enable us to see how *Felix Holt* partly regressed and yet largely advanced over the rhetorical techniques in *The Mill* and pushed on toward the new structure and techniques of *Middlemarch*.

It is a habit among critics to cleave this novel into the Holt and Transome sections, to throw away the worse part, and to discuss with pure ecstasy the other half. But a novel must be judged as a whole; a superb half can neither redeem the whole nor stand apart from it, and it may help to cause or explain the failure of the other half. Again, we must start with the critical question of what this novel, as a unity, is about.

If we read it as the story of Felix Holt's successful search for an adjustment of his personal and social values,[2] we must explain why nearly all emphasis is laid on Esther Lyon's change and on her inheritance, and why so much space is accorded to the Transome plot. If we accept the theory that the genesis of the novel was the tragedy of Mrs. Transome,[3] we must say that George Eliot's intentions changed. Mrs. Transome disappears from Chapter 9 to Chapter 34, so that her story is clearly not the central subject, though it is certainly more elaborated than necessary if it is only an appendage of the Felix-Esther plot.

A search for the connection of the two stories suggests another candidate for the central position in the novel. Esther's decision to renounce a life of ease is so climactic, so important for so many characters, and so thoroughly prepared as to suggest that *her* story is the subject and central interest of the novel. Certainly it is hard, under any other supposition, to justify the quantity of treatment she receives, the minute elaboration of her change of heart, the prominence of her father and her inheritance, or the obvious parallels between her and Mrs. Transome.

Nevertheless, Esther's story is tied to Felix's, and her ''conversion'' is for his happiness, so that we are forced to speak of the Esther-Felix and Transome plots and conclude that George Eliot was attempting to make a unity out of two sets of events of unequal proportions, which would allow her to explore ''the private lot of a few men and women . . . determined by a wider public life'' and the ''mutual influence of dissimilar destinies.''[4] This influence, presumably, would lead to integration of public and private lots in Felix and Esther as each recognizes his/her personal deficiency and supplies it through the other. The Transomes would fail of this integration, but would, by the warning vision of their lives, facilitate the success of the hero and heroine. To achieve proper distancing in such a scheme is no small task. It demands a depth of treatment proportioned to the importance of each event and its personages, close interconnections to make the two parts a unity and to support interest in each during its off-stage period, and enough similarity in narrative technique to allow the parts to coalesce.

Yet critical opinion maintains almost unanimously that the two plots do not blend and that the Felix-Esther plot is a failure. The two most frequently alleged causes for the failure are the politics and the complications over Esther's birth and inheritance. These events, like any others, should be so placed in relation to other events and just so much elaborated as to elucidate the characters' inner developments and struggles. They should not become a distracting interest or a plot puzzle on their own while the main characters are left in a temporary stasis.

Excessive use of topical politics can hardly be denied. Much of Mr. Lyon's discourse on political compromise and the secret ballot (chap. 16) must be as boring to the reader as to Harold Transome, while Felix's speech at the nominations (chap. 30) adds nothing to our knowledge of him, and that of his nameless predecessor comes from a character with no other appearance or function; these speeches represent an intrusion of politics for its own sake.

Nevertheless, the overflow of politics is not great enough to damage the rhetoric seriously. A fair amount of it would be needed in any case to specify Felix's background, which is barely presented any other way, since he is seen only once at home and never at work or church. The treating scene in Chapter 11, by its vigorous and dramatized contrast of Felix to Johnson, Chubb, and the colliers, successfully embodies in speaking individuals the social classes and issues that are the setting for Felix's life and development. Similarly, the market dinner in Chapter 20 exposes the fatuous ignorance of the satin-stock class that Felix refuses to join and to which he opposes his ideal. These amusing chapters are not without function, even though their plot connection is slight or nil.

But there is no question about the damage to the rhetoric done by the rigmarole of Esther's inheritance. Ten chapters,' often fairly long ones, deal almost exclusively with the intrigue to reveal her birth and rights, while several others deal with it in substantial part, and the entire fiasco of Mr. Lyon's debate (chaps. 15, 23, 24) is staged apparently for no other purpose than to reveal Esther's identity to Christian.[6] The whole parcel of coincidences and gross improbabilities[7] relates to the inheritance; these violate the otherwise sharp realism of the novel and presume on the reader's credulity to the extent of rousing his resentment and alienating his interest.

This damage is compounded by the complications introduced to insure legality. George Eliot's orginal sketch of Esther's claim (*GEL*, 4:216) was relatively clear and simple; unfortunately, she felt obliged to consult Frederic Harrison, who advised her to avoid the ''statute of limitations'' on the duration of such a claim by the use of a ''base fee'' (*GEL*, 4:217), which meant that Durfeys had to be added to Transomes and Bycliffes and old Tommy Trounsem had to be invented.[8] The puzzled and irritated reader is apt to be further confused by the issue of Harold's illegitimacy. It would be a safe guess that most readers at first assume that this fact is the basis for Esther's title, while in fact old Trounsem's death would make the estate revert to her whether Harold was legitimately born or not. But while we check and recheck and puzzle over all this, Felix and Esther are offstage, their character development is relegated to the back of our minds, and our personal interest in them is proportionately cooled.

These artificialities also cause minor characters to be developed and displayed out of all proportion to their function in the whole. Tommy Trounsem is a mere legal excrescence of the plot; Christian exists only to produce evidence of Esther's paternity. Johnson as agent of the treating at Sproxton would have some brief business relative to Felix, but his particular turpitude is overextended for the destruction of Jermyn's machinations with the inheritance. Had Mr. Lyon not required a romantic past, he would not have required so much space for fears and dubieties about it and could have served simply as the realistic and sympathetic embodiment of the lower-middle-class pole of Esther's choice.

It is true, of course, that Esther's choice demands some

possibilities of Transome Court and luxury as the other pole, and it is not easy to envision Harold's wooing her without some plot machination to make her a lady by birth. Fortunately, we are not obliged to decide how else George Eliot could have written her novel, but we are justified in saying that if she had wished her readers to be profoundly involved with the interior life of Esther and her lover, she should have managed to avoid so many external incidents and coincidences.

The plottedness of *Felix Holt* was criticized from the very beginning, but Dallas defended George Eliot by insisting that "she fulfils every requirement when she has succeeded, as we admit, in thoroughly awakening an interest in her tale. She enlists our sympathies in the lives of her characters . . . we care for them as if they were our intimate friends . . . ."[9] In modern terms, Dallas is saying that the failure in rhetoric of events is compensated by a successful rhetoric of character.

However, no critics except her contemporaries have ever admitted that George Eliot enlisted their sympathy or intimate care for Felix Holt. He is a bore, as only the intensely self-assured can be bores. Yet, like Adam Bede, he could have been educated out of his illusions and stuffiness by an engrossing process of conflict, suffering, and enlightenment. Had this been done, he could, as he should, have equaled Esther in interest and sympathy and been to readers an acceptable match for her. As it is, she accepts him, and the narrator tells us why, but we do not see *in him* reasons to satisfy us. It is not the whole Felix-Esther plot that fails, but the characterization of Felix, and that not in conception but in technique.

Felix's mother is quite right in saying that he "uses dreadful language." It is dreadful in both its content and its inaccurate representation. It is repellingly self-congratulatory: "I heeded not the candle, sir. I thank Heaven I am not a mouse to have a nose that takes note of wax or tallow"; it is sweepingly contemptuous of "your ringed and scented men of the people," "most of the preachers," "most of the middle class," the Dissenters, and a dozen other categories of men and women (chap. 5, passim). His speech is too loaded with stilted phrases and odd analogies to seem spontaneous and natural: a fine lady's notions are "about as applicable to the business of life as a pair of tweezers to the clearing of a forest" (1:105, chap. 5). His thought patterns are no better:

> Now by what fine meshes of circumstance did that queer devout old man, with his awful creed, which makes this world a vestibule with double doors to hell, and a narrow stair on one side whereby the thinner sort may mount to heaven—by what subtle play of flesh and spirit did he come to have a daughter so little in his own likeness? (1:109, chap. 5)

No consciousness in the world ever streamed like that. How can any reader be expected to relate closely to its owner?

Yet Felix's pompous moralizing would be tolerable, even interesting as consistent with his character, if only the narrator interpreted it as a fault we shall see him outgrow, not something we are currently expected to admire. It is the case of Adam Bede all over again, only worse, for the narrator of *Felix Holt* seems even more lacking in mental distance and discriminating judgment about the hero. In Felix's first visit to Lyon, the joke, as the narrator implies through viewpoint and diction, is not on the rude and vociferous Felix, but on the little minister:

> Mr Lyon was silent a few moments. This dialogue was far from plain sailing; he was not certain of his latitude and longitude. If the despiser of Glasgow preachers had been arguing in favour of gin and Sabbath-breaking, Mr Lyon's course would have been clearer. . . . it would not be well to smile too readily at what seemed but a weedy resemblance of Christian unworldliness. On the contrary, there might be a dangerous snare in an unsanctified outstepping of average Christian practice. (1:93-94, chap. 5)

Of course, the narrator knows that "Felix Holt had his illusions, like other young men," but since "they were not of a fashionable sort" (1:196, chap. 11), they presumably are superior to anyone else's sane realism. Felix's very faults are somehow admirable, merely the rough edges of his virtues; his blasphemous iconoclasm is rooted in his "large veneration" (1:198, chap. 5), and the narrator does not seem to see that joke as well as Felix himself does. No touch of that narrative irony by which George Eliot needles her faulty people ever pricks Felix. When he is somewhat shaken and unsure of himself after the love scene in Chapter 32, we are told:

> Felix wished Esther to know that her love was dear to him as the beloved dead are dear. He felt that they must not marry—that they would ruin each other's lives. But he had longed for her to know fully that his will to be always apart from her was renunciation, not an easy preference. In this he was thoroughly generous. (2:113, chap. 32)

And the narrator really believes it. No benevolent humor, no delicate barbs puncture Felix's erroneous views of his position, his gross analogy for Esther's love, or his downright fatuity about his distinguished celibacy.

Felix's ridiculous self-assurance could have become a source of interest when it began to totter from the concussion of his new love for Esther. But it is nearly impossible to sympathize deeply with his conflict, for there is almost no evidence of it.

Externally, there are too few events, and they reveal too little. Though the titular hero of the novel, Felix makes only eleven major appearances in its entire course.[10] To compensate for this scarcity (chiefly caused by all the inheritance maneuvers), these scenes would have to be highly dramatic and revealing, productive of powerful sympathy with the struggling young man. They simply are not. For example, his opening of his feeling and hopes to Esther during their walk in the fields (chap. 27) could have been a profoundly moving scene, but it fails for lack of any sense of pent-up passion or undiscovered depths in Felix. Though he talks of his inability to be just the man he wants to be, he at once speaks again as if his course were so clear and absolute that he could not fail to follow it. We have more of his exhortation, more of his simplistically clear view of his destiny, more of his everlasting calm and self-possession. Again, in Chapter 32, when Felix is finally wrought up, "at variance with himself," and unable to finish a sentence, and when the reader is worked up with him, Esther drops what should have been an emotional explosive: "What you have chosen to do has only convinced me that your love would be the better worth having" (2:111). And at this point, the agitated hero suddenly looks at her "with calm sadness," kisses her hand, and replies, "This thing can never come to me twice over. It is my knighthood. That was always a business of great cost" (2:112). Cold diction drenches our sympathy, which promptly fizzles out.

George Eliot might have allowed Felix his external self-control if she had permitted the reader to view the storm within. The single most serious flaw in *Felix Holt the Radical*, a defect far more ruinous to the novel's overall interest than even the politics and legal complications, is the minimal representation of Felix's mind and feelings. Of his eleven major appearances, the majority are narrated almost exclusively from Esther's viewpoint, and one each from Mr. Lyon's and Harold's. Even when an event is recorded through Felix's view, the narrator's language forms an elaborate rhetorical shield to deflect the force of Felix's own thoughts. As the election rioters rush toward Treby Manor, Felix reflects that:

> very unpleasant consequences might be hanging over him of a kind quite different from inward dissatisfaction; but it was useless now to think of averting such consequences. . . . his very movement seemed to him only an image of the day's fatalities, in which the multitudinous small wickednesses of small selfish ends, really undirected towards any larger result, had issued in widely-shared mischief that might yet be hideous. (2:127-28, chap. 33)

It is also useless to think of feeling closely Felix's pressure and vexation when his emotion is recorded by such elegant diction, sentence structure, and circumlocution.

The scenes with Esther particularly suffer for lack of an inside view of Felix's mind. Without that, we cannot be sure what complexities of response exist there and whether or not he is aware of them. When he deliberately comes to visit and lecture Esther in Chapter 10, his words suggest plainly that he is beginning to love her. But otherwise we can only speculate how much he is motivated by pure concern for her character, how much by unacknowledged desire to be with her, how much by irritation at finding himself falling in love with her. And we cannot sympathize fully with motives we do not know.

At times the lack of insight into Felix's mind can cause positive errors about him. In Chapter 18 Esther is mortified that Felix "evidently avoided coming to the house when she was there. . . . Of course, it was because he attributed such littleness to her that he supposed she would retain nothing else than a feeling of offence . . ." (1:292). The reader assumes with some reason that Felix's motive is a felt need to avoid the entanglement to which his emotions are leading him. But in Chapter 22 we are let briefly into his mind and there discover that "Felix had not thought the more of Esther because of that Sunday afternoon's interview. . . . He had avoided intruding on Mr Lyon without special reason, because he believed the minister to be preoccupied with some private care" (1:341). So there has been no conflict, no struggle, after all.

Yet we are later given to understand that Felix *has* in fact "had a horrible struggle" (2:295, chap. 45) against his growing love, and that during his incarceration "the wicked tempter" has been "snarling that word failure" (2:292) to make him surrender the purpose of his renunciation. Presumably, then, Felix has had two major periods of mental adjustment, before and during his imprisonment. Since these periods would necessarily occur when he is apart from Esther, we can know nothing about them except by views inside his mind. These we do not get. In particular, the complete blank on his prison experience deprives us of any sense of his "conversion" to an awareness of his own need for personal as well as social fulfillment. For all we know, he emerges from prison as convinced as ever of his self-sufficiency, and we feel that the happy duet of Chapter 51 can be formed only because Esther has learned to harmonize with Felix, not because there has been any corresponding change in him, or even any need for it.

Nor, in the end, does Felix have any evident social function, except to stay poor and presumably form more night schools, although all the ''horrible struggle'' in which we have been supposed to take so much interest was directed to the preservation of his great social aims against corruption by feminine pettiness. In Henry James's apt phrase, ''We find him a Radical and we leave him what?—only 'utterly married.' ''[11] But since events have led us to except something more than domestic happiness for Felix, we feel finally that we have been built up only for an unjust letdown.

The great anomaly of this novel is that Felix should be such a waste of possibilities while Esther, on the whole, is a triumph. She is admittedly not George Eliot's most exciting heroine; she is not so passionate and subject to inner strife as Maggie Tulliver, not so unmixedly egoistic as Rosamond Vincy, nor so psychologically complex as Dorothea Brooke. But while Maggie and Rosamond show the results of their unalterable natures, Esther actually undergoes a change, one more far-reaching than Dorothea's and more satisfactory in its results. Felix, however graceless, is more masculine and hence a more acceptable mate than Ladislaw, and Esther does not seem to have compromised any larger, nobler possibilities. In Esther's change George Eliot has successfully created a mental action that both rouses and satisfies intellectual interest, moral sympathy, and practical judgment.

The only severe damage to our interest in and sympathy for Esther is done by a backlash from the portrayal of Felix. Without sympathy for him, we can scarcely believe she would fall in love with him. Though we might believe she is frightened away from luxury by the unhappy Transomes, she would not be convincingly pulled toward Felix's poverty. Nevertheless, I think we do believe that Esther truly loves Felix and is changed under his influence. This credence is a tribute to the excellence of her portrait, which is technically almost the reverse of his.

Where Felix floats almost free of his background, Esther is

firmly placed in two realistic and opposed settings that concretize her choices and reveal the changes needed in her character. Though the narrator knows that Esther is too fastidious, her descriptions of Malthouse Yard justify her discriminations. She does live in a cramped and ugly house in a drab district among ignorant people, with a ridiculous maid and a father who is hard to listen to. The reader must understand how hard it will be to choose a life similar to this, how strong must be the love enabling the choice.

Mr. Lyon epitomizes Malthouse Yard and so serves as a touchstone for evaluating Esther's faults and basic virtues and the progress of her reformation. As the impassioned lover of an exiled, destitute, and widowed *belle dame*, Lyon is an unreal creation. But as the small, shortsighted preacher of orotund phrases, dubious exegesis, and unquestionable sincerity and zeal, he is completely credible and a genuinely felt obligation on Esther's and the reader's sympathetic understanding. He is best of all as the tender and timid father who veils the bust of the "eminent George Whitfield" because Esther cannot bear his squint, and who dares not press an investigation of her reading matter (1:101-6, chap. 5). It is in these little home episodes that Esther's princess-and-the-pea character is best realized. Her principal flaw is not her desire for lovelier surroundings or more intelligent companions; it is insensitivity to her tiresome but loving and gracious stepfather. Consequently, though we follow sympathetically her mind's submission to Felix's influence, we feel its results most keenly not when she accepts him as husband, but when she offers sudden demonstrations of love and service and appreciation to Mr. Lyon.

As Malthouse Yard concretizes Esther's role as princess in exile, so Transome Court does the refinement of luxury and of pain to which she will fall heir if she chooses it. These must be thoroughly specified for us if we are to feel the full force of her temptation and the particular virtue of her choice. So we are given the pleasure grounds with vistas of river and trees (2:271, chap. 43), the elegance of the refurbished house with its full squad of servants (2:134, chap. 34), and Esther herself in a new cashmere dress and wonderfully becoming turquoise ornaments (2:212, chap. 40); but we also get our first long look at ''feeble-minded, timid, paralytic,'' old Mr. Transome, who ''had never been part of the furniture she had imagined for the delightful aristocratic dwelling in her Utopia'' (2:209), and at the 1800 portrait of Mrs. Transome, urging the contrast between the brilliant young woman and the joyless, embittered, old one (2:237, chap. 42; 2:332-33, chap. 49).

The two richly detailed settings depict the two sides of Esther's character and the terms of her choice, but our sympathy with her choosing flows most of all from our close observation of the girl herself. Where scanty external views of Felix left us wondering what he really felt, Esther's changing attitudes amid her continuing sensibilities are perfectly displayed in small, apt details like her remaining at home amid the offensive lingering odors of dinner on the bare hope that Felix might call (2:30-31, chap. 27). Her great dramatic scenes are not of actions but of conversation, and her talk, unlike Felix's, is perfectly natural in form and expressive of spontaneous feeling. We can ally ourselves with the woman reacting indignantly to Felix's ill-bred lecture, yet simultaneously listen with some detached amusement to her painful defensive sparring.

When observation does not reveal enough about Esther, the narrator moves inside her mind, exposes her thoughts, and intertwines them with her own additional information or explanation. Seldom does this degenerate into a lengthy discourse on the obvious; rather, it reveals the intricacies of Esther's agitated psyche:

> Had he ever for a moment imagined that she had thought of him in the light of a man who would make love to her? . . . But did he love her one little bit, and was that the reason why he wanted her to change? Esther felt less angry at that form of freedom; though she was quite sure that she did not love him . . . . For the first time in her life Esther felt herself seriously shaken in her self-contentment. She knew there was a mind to which she appeared trivial, narrow, selfish. . . . Was it

> true that [her father's] life was so much worthier than her
> own? She could not change for anything Felix said, but she
> told herself he was mistaken if he supposed her incapable of
> generous thoughts. (1:188-89, chap. 10)

These thoughts prepare, as Esther's words alone would not, for her first unwonted display of tender affection to Lyon.

When Esther's thoughts will not explain her actions, the narrator gives the reader the benefit of her superior understanding of what to expect. After Esther has concluded that "she could not possibly call at Mrs Holt's" because all possible devices are "so transparent as to be undignified," the narrator adds, "but at the last moment there is always a reason not existing before—namely, the impossibility of further vacillation" (1:331, chap. 22). These passages reveal a narrator who is firmly and justly critical yet sympathetic. She displays neither waspish annoyance, as toward Hetty Sorrel, indiscriminate pity, as toward Maggie Tulliver, nor indiscriminate tolerance, as toward Felix. Esther's beauty does not irritate, and her defects are tolerated in the sure hope of her improvement. On such rhetorical guidance the reader may rely. Only once does George Eliot blunder badly in the narrative handling of Esther's view. When her growing impulse to testify for Felix is being recorded from within her mind, the narrator interrupts the swift current of her thought and deflects its force on the reader by a sentimentalized peroration:

> When a woman feels purely and nobly, that ardour of hers
> which breaks through formulas too rigorously urged on men
> by daily practical needs, makes one of her most precious in-
> fluences: she is the added impulse that shatters the stiffening
> crust of cautious experience. Her inspired ignorance gives a
> sublimity to actions so incongruously simple, that otherwise
> they would make men smile. Some of that ardour which has
> flashed out and illuminated all poetry and history was burning
> to-day in the bosom of sweet Esther Lyon. In this, at least, her
> woman's lot was perfect: that the man she loved was her hero;
> that her woman's passion and her reverence for rarest
> goodness rushed together in an undivided current. And to-day

they were making one danger, one terror, one irresistible impulse for her heart. (2:313, chap. 46)

The trite, formulaic diction, the inflated comparisons, and the cumbersome syntax do nothing to elevate the girl from Malthouse Yard into a heroine of romance, but they do break the momentum and change the tone of the scene, and on these factors depended our sense of Esther's pressuring love.

But the very rarity of such passages testifies to the superiority of the habitual delineation of Esther. If the narrator had done as well by Felix, we would have no problem with him, or with Esther's final resolution to forgo wealth in the hope of having his love. It is no weakness in the depiction of Esther that prevents our full sympathy with her decision, but only in that of Felix, especially Felix as opposed to Harold and Mrs. Transome, the rival claimants for Esther's love and tender attention.

The Transomes are not merely bundles of functions relative to Esther and Felix. As principals of the subplot, they illustrate how the inevitable interlocking of public and private deeds can bring the selfish to grief, and therefore they must exist as vividly for the reader as for Esther. On the other hand, they are in a *sub*plot and so cannot exist in narrative disregard of Felix and Esther, but only in a manner that reflects clearly the lovers' alternate possible selves. Mrs. Transome exists artistically to exhibit a life poisoned by private self-gratification, Harold to be a pseudo-politician whose public value is spoiled by his personal selfishness, as Felix fears his could be. As Felix's rival, he must be reasonably attractive to Esther and to the reader, but never so much as to shake the reader's desire for the actual outcome. We must pity the Transomes' suffering, but we must never be more seriously involved with either of them than with Felix and Esther, and we must never want Esther to join them.

That the Transomes are painted vividly and successfully is acknowledged by every critic of this novel. Except for Maggie Tulliver, Mrs. Transome is the most complex character George Eliot had yet drawn; and her anguish is at once the most thoroughly depicted and, *in itself*, the most perfectly distanced emotion yet presented to the reader's compassionate understanding. The narrator has so clear a view of Mrs. Transome's life, both internal and external, that he can present it with clean lines of description, dialogue, or thought, and with little or no insistence on its meaning or its claim on the reader's sympathy.

Description in the first chapter engages the reader and reveals the life and personality of the woman through small, cogent details about her appearance, her opinions on various subjects, and her behavior to tenants and laborers. In the face of these details, which brand the woman as a superficial mind and a petty tyrant, the narrator preserves sympathy by his omniscient notation of "the full truth," that Mrs. Transome has "a woman's keen sensibility and dread . . . behind all her petty habits and narrow notions" and has endured "long painful years" burdened with "crosses, mortifications, money-cares, conscious blameworthiness" and "advancing age" (1:42-43). Of course, this is not yet the "full truth" about her blameworthiness, but we must see and hear more of her and of the characters around her before we are ready to react with intelligent sympathy to that revelation.

Most of Mrs. Transome's thoughts and speeches are quite brief, but her fewest words or the slightest notations of her thought usually suffice for accurate representation and utmost poignancy. When Jermyn has threatened Harold and left the house with a deliberate pretense of not seeing his mother, we are told that "she heard the voices of Mr Transome and little Harry at play together. She would have given a great deal at this moment if her feeble husband had not always lived in dread of her temper and her tyranny, so that he might have been fond of her now" (2:147, chap. 35). When her maid finds her after the revelation, she cries, "No, I am not ill. I am not going to die! I shall live—I shall live!" Not all Adam Bede's fevered raving approaches the power of this utmost expression of agony, nor could a lengthy dialogue render more yearning than does the one command, ". . . leave me. . . . It may be that my son will come to me" (2:344-45, chap. 50). George Eliot had now achieved the ability to enter a mind and heart so deeply and yet objectively that she could render its depths in single phrases that shake us by what they disclose.

George Eliot carefully gauges the pity and severity due Mrs. Transome by the use of the subordinate characters around her. Because her husband has always been half idiot and her legitimate son just like him, we can at least understand her capitulating to a handsome "soft-glancing, versifying young Jermyn" (2:325, chap. 47), who could give her homage and a healthy heir; but at present she repels us by her Medusa-like power to paralyze the old man with fear and spoil his harmless pleasures (1:18-19, chap. 1). The moral vulgarity and cruel indifference of Jermyn rouse a compassion for the woman who cannot now rid herself of his presence or his constricting power over her psyche and her property; by comparison with him, she seems a noble victim. Yet we must believe she earned her misery by willful blindness to the rapacity that must have lurked behind the soft words and glances. Indeed, it is difficult to believe that Jermyn was ever really attractive. Rhetorically, he is the least effective character in the Transome plot, too much a machinating stage villain in middle-class vesture to fit well into a realistic novel. But he is most "felt" in the scenes with Mrs. Transome. The one that would most readily descend to melodrama, his demand that she tell Harold his paternity, comes off successfully because Mrs. Transome's lashing speeches are free of sentimentality and have a credible intensity and phraseology.

As Mrs. Transome's tragic disappointment and as our gauge to sympathy for her, Harold Transome needs to be presented clearly but not at great length. Few portions of the novel surpass the dramatization of his insensibility to his mother's feelings, displayed in his blunt announcement of his Radicalism, his tactless comments on the deterioration of the furniture and on English wives, his regret at his servant's delay ("for I shall have nobody to cook for me"), and his "kind" intent to reduce his mother to a "grandmamma on satin cushions" (1:21-28, chap. 1). The rhetoric of dialogue here generates keen pity for Mrs.

Transome, but it is mitigated by previous evidence that she would truly devour and dominate Harold if he let her and that she is reaping what she sowed, selfishness in a son to whom she could scarcely impart anything else.

Yet Harold is not merely crass or brutal. It is just the bitterest irony of Mrs. Transome's retribution that Harold's feeling for her aggravates his anger against Jermyn and thus urges him to the very action that will cause the pain she dreads. In the scene in which Jermyn announces his fatherhood (chap. 47), all the elements are selected to make sympathy cling strongly to Harold: the ironic expansion on his good humor and self-satisfaction, the opprobrious metaphors for Jermyn as a wild animal at bay and a fanged snake, Jermyn's past slimy conduct and his present iniquity in publicly obliterating Mrs. Transome's reputation, and the kindly reaction of Sir Maximus.[12] The melodrama that could easily have seized on this scene is forestalled by its rapid pace, minimal narrative, and terse dialogue, which generate a force of pity for Harold and sympathy with his revulsion that carry us safely through his temporary hardness to his mother. The reader shares profoundly Esther's pity for both the suffering Transomes and thus is equally grateful for the resolution afforded each of them, a new fellow-feeling and compassion in Harold, love and release from fear for Mrs. Transome.

But whatever enthusiasm the private Transome story rouses, one must ask if it functions adequately either in the social picture that the whole novel is to convey or in the Esther-Felix story. In the first case, public circumstances should affect Mrs. Transome's private sorrow; likewise, her past should presumably have some social repercussions; and this interaction should considerably stimulate our interest in both.

Chapter 3 lists the specific results of political conditions that will affect the Transome destinies: Harold's candidacy, Jermyn's affability with Lyon, and the use of damningly suggestive handbills (1:73). Harold's declaring as a Radical puts Jermyn into contact with the minister of like political color, and this puts him into possession of information with which he can threaten Harold. But some potential for conflict and interest is wasted here, for Harold is never really forced to make the choice Jermyn thrusts upon him. He is mentally and morally torn over the issue until, "as the temptation to avoid all risk of losing the estate grew and grew . . . the difficulty of bringing himself to make a compact with Jermyn seemed more and more insurmountable" (2:151, chap. 36). At this crucial and fascinating point, enter Christian with the information, partly gained through the handbills (2:69-71, chap. 29), that will save Harold the necessity of a full moral choice. Thus, not only do Jermyn's machinations and our interest come to nothing, but so also does the main connection between Harold's birth and his politics.

For it cannot be said that his public Radicalism has any other notable impact on his or his mother's private lives. It is part of her general disappointment in him, but that would have been keen enough in any case, and both apparently forget it once he has lost the election. Nor does the secret past have any evident social implications except the bare suggestion that the scurrilous placards may have helped lose Harold the election. Illegitimacy does not evidently affect his social life or status as a landholder, even after it becomes public knowledge, beyond a discreet and temporary absence from home (Epilogue). In short, by drawing so many threads, public and private, onto her story loom, George Eliot rendered herself unable to weave them all together and to make each one contribute to the interest we take in the other and in all combined.

But though Harold's electioneering is barefly functional in guiding readers' reaction to him or his mother, it has another function in the Felix-Esther plot—namely, to make him an un-sympathetic foil to Felix. Harold's motive for seeking office is essentially to gratify his private ambition for public status and power; he deplores any disgraceful methods of canvassing but is unwilling to restrain his agents. This sets him up in a scene of diametric opposition to Felix (chaps. 16 and 17), so that his weakness of character may the more impress us with Felix's unbending probity and pure zeal for public improvement. In the plot stucture, the objectionable treating with liquor also leads to Felix's ill-fated role in the riot, so that the entire affair becomes

known to Esther, who is just then in a position to choose one of
them as lover.

Here, as foil and rival to Felix in love, is Harold's main function in the novel and here also is—or should be—his mother's.
Unless the two plots can coalesce here, they simply fly apart and
destroy the novel's unity. Hence it is absolutely necessary that
Harold and his mother be so distanced as to make us feel their
vital and compelling magnetism for Esther, yet also make us
desire her final decision in their regard.

Esther's attraction to Harold as opposed to Felix is one of the
best-handled features of the novel.

As a well-meaning but morally mediocre suitor, Harold is a
great improvement over Stephen Guest. There is enough physical
description to make us feel his pleasing masculine presence and
enough dramatized evidence of his real deference to and roused
interest in Esther to explain her inevitable delight. And George
Eliot is scrupulously true to human nature in representing
Esther's reactions, her inclination to marry Harold and her irritation at Felix's assumption that she will do so (2:228, chap. 41),
her alternations between shame and pride in Felix, fascination
with and distaste for Harold, delight in and moral rejection of ease
and luxury. For the greater portion of nine chapters[13] we dwell inside Esther's embattled mind, feeling the full strength of her pen-
chant for Harold and the life he offers and her sense of his moral
inferiority to Felix. By the very force that her thoughts and vi-
sions have for her, we feel the rightness of the decisions she draws
from them.

This intense concentration on Esther does remove us wholly
from the jailed Felix, with unfortunate effects on his characterization, as already noted. But it is the reader, not Esther or Harold,
who needs to see more of Felix in this crucial period. That the
competition between Felix and Harold is registered simply in
Esther's reactions to each of them is perfectly appropriate, since
the real test for her is how well she has absorbed Felix's principles
and how well they will stand up in his absence and in the uncertainty of reward. His continuous presence in her thoughts is

enough to make us feel his power over her. The real reason why the concentration on Esther should be balanced with views of Felix in prison is that without these we do not sensibly comprehend his need for her as antidote to the needs of Harold and especially his mother.

For Esther's is not the only mind we see in these chapters. The courtship observed from Harold's vantage takes on a piquancy for the reader as much as for the suitor. It is pleasantly amusing to see him pricked with interest in Esther, stimulated by the sense of difficulties in wooing her, fatuously confident that "Felix Holt could not be his rival in any formidable sense" (2:322, chap. 47). Simply because we enter Harold's viewpoint, we take a lively interest in his prospects.

Still, we would never want Esther to marry the complacent, indifferently good-natured Harold. But when his complacency is shattered by Jermyn's announcement, when he knows his lowered status "in the eyes of the world," and when he determines to do at any cost "what he knew that perfect honour demanded" (2:334-35, chap. 49), then the inside account of his mind and motives shows a new and a profoundly sympathetic Harold Transome whose deep inner need Esther could fill. Esther herself feels a pity for him "so strong, that it spread itself like a mist over all previous thought and resolve"—and over any resolve the reader has in Felix's favor. It is a fine insight into Esther's psychology to note that "with a paradoxical longing . . . she wished at that moment that she could have loved this man with her whole heart" (2:337); the trouble is that the reader is apt, by this time, to wish it also. And when Harold goes to his anguished mother with tenderness and pardon, thus demonstrating that he has accepted Esther's lesson of love, it is hard not to feel that he deserves to win her.

If this is true of Harold's need for Esther, how much more so of Mrs. Transome's! The new interest and happiness that she receives from Esther's company are repeatedly urged on our notice, and she herself expresses several times her wish to have Esther as a daughter (2:212, chap. 40; 2:289, chap. 45). It is difficult at that point not to identify with her wish; it is virtually impossible after we have seen her crushed by Jermyn's disclosure and Harold's severity, after we have seen her pride give way to loneliness and longing for Esther's pitying love, after we have heard her poignant response to receiving it: ''God has some pity on me'' (2:348, chap. 50). We know of no need of Felix's that can compare with this one; indeed, it has been part of Esther's trouble that Felix ''always seemed to her too great and strong to be pitied: he wanted nothing'' (2:177, chap. 37). But Mrs. Transome wants badly a loving daughter to be with her and to compensate Harold for his sorrow. When Esther says to Harold, ''I think I would bear a great deal of unhappines to save her from having any more'' (2:350, chap. 50), she means it as a plea to him; but one cannot help reflecting that her marrying into this house would be no longer a surrender to ease but could be interpreted as a noble self-giving for the very purpose she has stated.

Obviously, George Eliot never intended us to feel any discontent with the actual outcome of the novel. That we do feel it is not attributable to any dissatisfaction with her moral plan or any real desire for Esther to marry an inferior man whom she does not thoroughly love. Rather, our unease is due to the technical imbalance in characterization. Mrs. Transome is too strong not only for Felix, but for the novel as a whole. A brilliant creation in herself, she becomes a wedge sundering the work into its uneven parts.

In conclusion, it may be said that the novel's deficiencies in distancing, in maneuvering the degrees of sympathetic involvement with the characters, are attributable mainly to poorly managed rhetoric of event and character. Too many events are cumbersome and unhelpful in the progress of the characters and do not reflect light or interest on each other. Too many characters are unbalanced in their rhetorical relationship: Mrs. Transome's only large function is to be Esther's ''vision,'' yet she usurps most of the interest; the least engrossing character is he who is to be Esther's husband and happiness. Even minor characters like Mr. Lyon, Mrs. Holt, and Christian stand out to the life and Felix pales by comparison.

Yet, with all its faults, *Felix Holt the Radical* has excellences that merit it more serious consideration than it has usually received from George Eliot readers. There is, after all, something to be said for the pleasure of brilliant parts, even if they cannot make a perfectly compacted whole; Mrs. Transome and Esther are worth knowing. George Eliot also displays here a greatly increased control and sophistication in the rhetoric of language and narration. There are some lumpish sentences and wearying longueurs, some indigestible parts of the story, such as those explaining the political or legal connivings. But ordinarily, the narrator of *Felix Holt* can fuse description and judgment in a terse expression, applying a cool irony to persons and situations, such as the publican Chubb with his "political 'idee,' which was, that society existed for the sake of the individual, and that the name of that individual was Chubb" (1:193, chap. 11). George Eliot is approaching the creation of that restrained yet concerned person with the world-voice who will narrate *Middlemarch*.

Further, *Felix Holt* is noteworthy for the possibilities it presents, even if these are not fully realized. It is a profitable experiment in the use of a double plot and indicates that with improved techniques to interlock the halves, a good whole can be constructed. The possibility of such a whole depends largely on the further possibility of a richly textured social picture compounded from fully realized and well distanced characters and issues, together with a chorus of individuals briefly but sharply etched. Blackwood said that *Felix Holt* lacked "the ordinary Novel interest" but richly possessed that of "a series of panoramas where human beings speak and act before us" (*GEL*, 4:243); he was especially taken with the lifelikeness of the figures in the side scenes and of their speeches (*GEL*, 4:245). When George Eliot succeeded in imparting that same lifelikeness to her protagonists and in fusing her superb panoramas with the fictional interest of a story of human conflict and decision, she produced her master portrait of provincial society. *Felix Holt*, in short, is rich in all the possibilities of *Middlemarch*.

Notes

1. See Mary D. Springer, *Forms of the Modern Novella* (Chicago: University of Chicago Press, 1975), pp. 39-53; Wm. E. Buckler, "Memory, Morality and the Tragic Vision in the Early Novels of George Eliot," in *The English Novel in the Nineteenth Century: Essays on the Literary Mediation of Human Values*, ed. George Goodin (Urbana: University of Illinois Press, 1972), pp. 159-60.

2. David R. Carroll, "*Felix Holt*: Society as Protagonist," *Nineteenth Century Fiction* 17 (1962): 237-52.

3. Fred C. Thomson, "The Genesis of *Felix Holt*," *PMLA* 74 (1959): 576-84. George Eliot's original intentions cannot be determined from the *Letters* and *Journals*.

4. George Eliot, *Felix Holt the Radical*, Standard Edition in 2 vols. (Edinburgh: William Blackwood and Sons, 189-?), 1:72, chap. 3. As with the previous novels, citations refer first to volume and page of this edition and then to the chapter number for the benefit of users of other editions.

5. Chaps. 12, 13, 14, 21, 25, 28, 29, 35, 36, 37.

6. W. J. Harvey, *The Art of George Eliot* (New York: Oxford University Press, 1962), pp. 133-34, discusses what else George Eliot may have intended by the debate and why she cut it off. She should have cut it out.

7. Mr. Lyon's past history with Annette; Christian, Jermyn, and Lyon each having a piece of the story of the inheritance and all happening to come together at the same time and place after so many years; Christian's carrying the locket around with him and happening to lose it; Felix's finding it and scrupling to return it himself and happening to ask Lyon to do so; Christian's meeting Trounsem over the bill-sticking job; Christian's learning Johnson's identity through the chance of Felix's speech; Trounsem alone being killed out of all those rioting on election day.

8. We may at least be grateful that Harrison's further suggestion for making Esther a true Transome descendant as well as a Bycliffe was met by George Eliot with "disinclination to adopt this additional coincidence" and "artificiality of plot" (*GEL*, 4:228-31).

9. E. S. Dallas, *The Times*, 26 June 1886, reprinted in Gordon S. Haight, ed., *A Century of George Eliot Criticism* (Boston: Houghton Mifflin Co., 1965), p. 38.

10. Chaps. 5, 10, 16, 17, 22, 27, 30, 32, 33, 45, 46, 51. The distancing effect of this scarcity is aggravated by the fact, already noted, that Felix has no well-specified, personally identifying background of his own.

11. Henry James, "Felix Holt, the Radical," *The Nation*, 16 August 1866, reprinted in Haight, p. 40.

12. Perhaps it requires a fine sense of the meaning that *gentleman* conveys to the English to find any moral tone in Sir Maximus's ejection of Jermyn for violating a "meeting of gentlemen." But his act does enhance our sympathy for Harold.

13. Chaps. 38, 40, 41, 43-46, 49, 50.

[5]

Middlemarch

To arrive at *Middlemarch* is, by critical consensus, to arrive at George Eliot's peak. This is true, no matter what critical approach is used. From the formal-rhetorical perspective, *Middlemarch* seems her best example of fiction as "an arrangement of events or feigned correspondence according to predominant feeling" and of her own "conception of wholes composed of parts more and more multiplied and highly differed, yet more and more absolutely bound together by various conditions of common likeness or mutual dependence."[1] Into *Middlemarch* George Eliot put her greatest number of vocal and active characters and linked them by numerous parallels and contrasts in several principal and subordinate plots with such varied emotional effects as drawing room and ale-house comedy, serious pathos, and tragic pity. To pull all these elements together into any degree of formal unity and to achieve the predominant feeling that comes from unified theme and skillful rhetorical techniques must be a master's feat, and critics disagree on how well George Eliot accomplished it.

It is my position that *Middlemarch* is, indeed, George Eliot's best example of fictional rhetoric, because in it she mastered most of her earlier problems. She created a much more complex yet more coherent whole than ever before; she most successfully structured several related plots and proportioned the characters and episodes for rhetorical effect; she produced her most mature narrator, the best related to both characters and reader; and she finally produced one steady and almost wholly successful tragic plot. But I also recognize that the novel shows partial disunity in another plot and in the theme, a disruption of the intended whole, due to the rhetorically confused representation and interpretation of a beloved heroine—a problem of form and rhetoric as severe as any George Eliot ever displayed, one that she apparently could not master. Rhetorical analysis of the novel may be structured by an examination of those strengths and weaknesses.

The Whole: Subject and Theme

Analysis must begin, as always, with a description of the normative whole. With so much multiplicity and differentiation of parts, this whole can exist, if at all, only in terms of coherent subject and theme. Modern critics agree (and I concur) that the novel has unity, that its subject is an exploration of human aspiration and fulfillment as affected by personal potential and by individual and social influences, and that its theme is the minimal chances of success for uncommon people in a mediocre society. But beyond that consensus, critics disagree about how many plots there are (numerations range from one to five), who the protagonist(s) is (or are), how important the various stories are, how the theme applies to some of the characters, and whether the novel's ultimate effect is tragic or serious but positive.[2]

In my view, the subject of aspiration and fulfillment is embodied first in Dorothea and Lydgate as joint protagonists, centers of parallel main plots, designed to rouse similar kinds of sympathy as they aspire greatly and fail tragically. Neither one can be considered only as a principal figure in the other's story, as Tom Tulliver is in Maggie's; neither has so much influence on the other's life. Their stories run independently, with only two major crossings—in Casaubon's illness and Bulstrode's scandal. Lydgate's story is almost as long as Dorothea's (35 chapters to 42) and just as substantial. Whether or not the reader is meant to feel sympathetic liking for Lydgate as intensely as for Dorothea, he is clearly meant to give a parallel interest and importance to Lydgate's story and its meaning. Both protagonists have their potential hampered by personal flaws and social conditions that issue in a stultifying marriage, though Lydgate's failure is attributed chiefly to his flaws and Dorothea's chiefly to society. The great flaw in this design of parallel tragic failures is Dorothea's second marriage. The union itself would be no problem if it were clearly a second failure. Certainly it does not fulfill Dorothea's highest potential and aspirations; hence it maintains the parallel to Lydgate. But it does fulfill her aspiration for love, and it does give her much happiness; hence it does not fit into a pattern of tragedy or even of serious diminishment. The problem, however, as will be seen, is less in an overall pattern of action than in the thematic interpretation of Dorothea and Will and their marriage.

Both Lydgate and Dorothea are meant, I believe, to be seen as failing on a large scale of potential; Fred Vincy succeeds on a small one. He is the center of a subplot that reflects theirs in a reverse image. He is a foil to both of them and to his sister Rosamond in that his education to reality and to altruism comes soon enough to let him find his true potential and so achieve both success in a limited work and solid happiness in marriage. (In her second marriage, Dorothea looks more a parallel to him than to Lydgate.) The Garth family, Farebrother, and the Featherstone people all serve primarily our interest in Fred.

Bulstrode, I believe, is not properly a plot center, but a chief functionary in Lydgate's plot and a lesser in Fred's and Dorothea's. He functions in only ten chapters and has a "plot" only in the events that reveal his past. And that revelation serves primarily not to engage our practical concern for Bulstrode, but to incriminate Lydgate. In the structure of the whole, Bulstrode serves essentially as a social type and agent. He embodies or elicits the society's conflicting values regarding religion, medicine, money, status, and marriage, and he causes those values to become tests for Lydgate and others. In so comprehensive a novel, it is good to have one character who, more than all the choral figures, reveals the thoughts and motives at play in the background. But such a social person clearly should not draw excessive interest to his separate self.

Out of this story of great failures and lesser successes, a coherent theme does emerge. In a society of commonplace and egoistic values and aspirations, ordinary good people can achieve ordinary happiness (Fred Vincy); but uncommon people are liable to destruction or grave failure, either from their own ''spots of commonness'' reflecting society's (Lydgate) or from the commonness of the society that overpowers them (Dorothea). In such a society, the individual's best hope for giving and achieving happiness lies in a realistic altruism toward the nearest other persons; attempts to do good on a public scale are likely to fail. This theme emerges from the ignorance or wisdom of all the characters, from their morally negative or positive responses to their situations; and it can be turned back upon all of them as a vision of life by which we can interpret them and gauge our sympathy for them. It is, in fact, applied with great consistency to Lydgate and Fred Vincy and to all in their stories; and it is my contention that it is applied very successfully to Dorothea in the matter of her first marriage. But in her entire relation to Will Ladislaw, thematic unity is disrupted.

Incongruity exists first within the theme itself. In her illustrative function, Dorothea represents uncommon potential in her ardent and moral nature; her faults are the reverse effects of her virtues, and her grave failure is caused almost wholly by ''a society not made to second noble aspirations in a woman.''[3] The result is tragic unfulfillment of her nature in marriage (or total unfulfillment in one marriage and fulfillment as a lover but not as a whole person in the second). The rhetoric supports this illustrative function in the first marriage. But as interpreted by the rhetoric, the second marriage illustrates two conflicting themes: it is both the culmination of a glorious love story and an inadequate fate for Dorothea; she is both a great lover who heroically chooses another great lover, and she is an ardent but naïve woman trapped by lack of better options into choosing another second-rate husband. The ultimate thematic discrepancy, therefore, is that her choice of love, which is rhetorically glorified, is her tragic or near-tragic unfulfillment, which is rhetorically lamented.

That part of the theme which has Dorothea illustrate the un-common, heroically ardent lover is also in conflict with her mimetic representation, which fairly and accurately depicts her errors. She is not so uncommon as the theme requires; she has abundant personal folly, seen clearly in her estimate of both her husbands. The rhetoric alternately calls attention to Dorothea's folly and invites laughter, and then masks her folly and glorifies her for her ardor. (It does the same for Will.) This is partially true when she loves Casaubon, but emphatically true when Will is in-volved.

Small wonder, then, that even the earliest reviewers complained of a ''feeling of uncertainty and unsatisfiedness as to the whole fable and its impression which remains with the reader when all is done.''[4] In the end we do not know, and modern critics still can-not agree, whether to interpret the marriage as Dorothea's sec-ond error due to her idealizing another unworthy mate, as a regrettable but inevitable constriction of Dorothea due to social conditions, or as a generally wise and liberating choice that satisfies both Dorothea and George Eliot.[5] Though the Prelude seems to give the second interpretation very explicitly, it has not silenced debate, probably because it lies outside the story proper, where thematic confusion reigns.

Even though the Dorothea-Will story does not readily fit into a primarily tragic pattern, and even though that story's relation to the theme remains ambiguous, it is still true that *Middlemarch* does have a coherence and a wholeness that come from subject and theme. It is that otherwise striking wholeness which makes the one rupture so obvious and glaring. We do know what this novel is about and what it means. Subject and theme, as described, require a rhetoric that will consistently distance the characters according to their function in the plots and according to their positive or negative relation to the theme. We must sympathize if the characters have high aspiration and real potential for fulfilling it, if their achievement is actually and unjustly obstructed, and if they have genuine altruism or suffer much from others' egoism. Such a rhetorical prescription necessitates in turn a carefully designed structure, a narrator in control of her words, feelings, and judgment, and a representation of character and event that is consistent with the implied interpretation and can thereby induce the desired emotion. In attempting to fulfill these general requirements, George Eliot achieved her largest successes and met with her major failure. We must now turn to the specific techniques she used.

Structure

A novel requiring several coordinated plots to encompass its subject obviously requires also a most skillful structuring of the plots to control the reader's levels of interest and emotional response. In previous novels George Eliot either seemed to have a dual plot when she really did not (*Adam Bede* and *Mill on the Floss*) or actually did have one and was unable to meld the two parts into a unity (*Felix Holt*). We have seen that these failures in unification were due to failures in placing and proportioning events and characters, which failures in turn confused the distancing of many characters. But in *Middlemarch* George Eliot very nearly mastered the challenge of structuring the dual plot and subplot.

The first structural requirement is that Dorothea and Lydgate, as parallel protagonists, must each be solidly and soon enough established so that neither can prevent or diminish the other's hold on the reader's concern. Lydgate's early claim, however, is doubly endangered, by the Prelude and by the delay of his entry.

The Prelude apparently was intended for "Miss Brooke," a projected novel of which Dorothea was protagonist.[6] That George Eliot did not revise or eliminate it when she fused "Miss Brooke" with Lydgate's story (the original "Middlemarch")[7] is very unfortunate. For in the finished novel, the Prelude, more than any other element, sets up a false idea of the whole and a singleness of interest that must be overcome later. Without the Prelude these errors would be far less likely to occur, for the ending of Chapter 10 and the opening of Chapter 11 clearly imply that Lydgate is a strong new interest in the novel as in the town, that he is to have his own story of ambition and marriage, and that he and Dorothea will have no interest in each other until after a "slow preparation of effects from one life on another."[8]

But there is still a question whether Lydgate should not have been introduced sooner than Chapter 10.[9] By that time the reader is so engrossed in Dorothea that it is jolting to be pulled entirely away from her for a totally new interest. Had the whole novel's pattern been present to George Eliot from the start of her writing she might well have brought Lydgate in sooner and thereby made his role clearer and his early interest stronger. That interest is further diluted by immediate dramatizations of Rosamond and of the Vincy-Waule competition for Featherstone's money. Before Chapter 15 Lydgate is dramatized only twice and very briefly; not until then does he get the prominent position and detailed description due him as protagonist.

But once the protagonists are firmly established in our memories and imaginations, George Eliot makes frequent alternations between plots and subplots so that no area of interest is long unrepresented. A comparison of the present order of chapters with that first projected illuminates the rhetorical effect of these alternations. The original order was:

Chapters 23 – 25	Fred's horse trading and debt failure
19 – 22	Dorothea in Rome
28 – 30	Dorothea's misery at home, Casaubon's first illness, Will's invitation to the Grange
26 – 27	Fred's illness and attendance by Lydgate
31 – 33	Lydgate's engagement, Featherstone's death

This order, besides weakening interest in each plot by shelving it too long, would have made Dorothea's marriage and disillusionment and Casaubon's illness seem rushed; the same for Lydgate's flirtation and engagement. But we must feel a slow, monotonous misery in Dorothea's life and a slow, unrecognized entrapment occurring in Lydgate's.

There are, however, three noteworthy exceptions to these frequent alternations of the plots. Dorothea is absent from Chapters 11 through 18 and 63 through 75, with a brief reappearance in Chapter 72; Lydgate is offstage during Chapters 47 through 57, with only a brief showing in Chapter 50 to recommend Farebrother for Lowick parish. Dorothea first disappears in a glow of joyous idealism; she reappears in tears and disillusionment, thus jarring us into sympathy with her own emotional shock. Lydgate's disappearance prevents interruption of the emotional momentum of Casaubon's illness and death and Dorothea's rapid turning toward Will; also, by withholding Lydgate's crisis period until after the death of Casaubon, George Eliot avoided placing on the reader's sympathy the unsupportable burden of two oppressively unhappy situations together. Then when Lydgate the still-contented husband suddenly returns a miserable and heavily pressured man, we share his own shock at Rosamond and sense what he has been suffering during the interim away from us. Finally, Dorothea's second absence allows for a rapid accumulation of Lydgate's trouble with Rosamond and Bulstrode, making us feel the uninterrupted pressure as he feels it; thus Dorothea's faith in him rouses all the more sympathy for both of them when it comes.

The subplot of Fred Vincy would necessarily occupy much less space than the two main stories. In fact, Fred appears dramatically in only twelve chapters, is mentioned in eight others, and disappears for periods even exceeding fifteen chapters. Yet his story can still seem too detailed for its importance or inherent interest. This is not due to his too frequent presence but to an excess of the Featherstone-Waule grotesques and, above all, to Fred's lack of active connections to the two main plots. He never meets Dorothea or has any link to her story except that he works with Mr. Garth at Tipton and Freshitt and he could lose Mary when

Farebrother gets the Lowick living. These facts do almost nothing to point the analogy of his story to Dorothea's or to affect our interest in either her or him. In the Lydgate plot Fred has the family connection but little active part. His typhoid conveniently brings the doctor into the house, and he does stop Lydgate's gambling just when he himself has been tempted to start again, thus making the reverse image clearer. But that is all. Fred's story floats free of the main plots structures, leaving the reader to notice the analogies as he can. It has the interest of Fred's own character, and of the Garths' and Mr. Farebrother's, but for a fully appropriate rhetorical impact, it would need either to be developed as a third parallel plot with more drama of its own or else to be more clearly subordinated and closely linked to the plots it is supposed to reflect.

The one really grave flaw in the total structure of *Middlemarch* is the attempt to elaborate a mystery plot out of Bulstrode's past. Some secret guilt he must have, also a tangle of motivations around it, but not so many complications to reveal it or to engage the reader's fascination with his character. A vagrant like Raffles could wander naturally into a town the size of Middlemarch and find Bulstrode there; everything essential would follow. The needless Rigg connection generates needless scenes and improbable coincidences. And the Ladislaw involvement leads nowhere in the plot, is hardly significant even to the town gossip, reveals nothing new about Bulstrode, and has no real effect on Will's relation to Dorothea or on anyone else's reaction to him or Bulstrode. These complications simply call excess attention to Bulstrode beyond the limits of his function as a social symptom and agent, and they alienate the reader by straining his credulity. Bulstrode needs no special personal plot; he has ample connections to Lydgate's story, and his role as patron of the hospital seems enough link to Dorothea's.

The importance of developing and placing events for rhetorical impact applies not only to events within the novel time but to those outside that time range. In previous novels George Eliot did not use pre-novel events that required lengthy flashbacks (Thias

Bede's drinking and Mrs. Transome's adultery need no explanation). But in *Middlemarch* several characters have significant pasts that need flashback, and she began to use this device with considerable skill.

One of the best examples conditions our responses to Lydgate. Jerome Beaty offers evidence that Chapter 15 was originally the Introduction to "Middlemarch," the separate novel with Lydgate as hero. In revision, this chapter was placed after the initial complication with Rosamond.[12] This inversion has strong rhetorical effects. For in Chapter 15, the narrator, frankly claiming omniscience, proposes to "make the new settler Lydgate better known to anyone interested in him" and she asserts that the doctor is, indeed, "more uncommon than any general practitioner" (1:214-15). Then she flashes back to describe Lydgate's "call" to medicine in terms suggestive of the prophet's vocation: the youth and superiority of the one called, the total absence of any expectation of the call, the particularity of its moment and place, "the voices within," the kindled spark and sudden illumination from "the first passage that drew his eyes." "The moment of vocation had come, and before he got down from his chair, the world was made new to him. . . . From that hour Lydgate felt the growth of an intellectual passion" (1:216-18). This powerful, even biblical, language is then supported by accounts of his high-quality education in medicine, his human concern for patients, his zeal for social good and medical reform, the prudent planning and determined integrity of his practice. The total effect is utterly to convince the reader of the validity of Lydgate's medical vocation and of his potential to be a successor of Bichat. This passage conditions all our future reactions to him; it reechoes through every agonizing dialogue with Rosamond, through every narration of his money worries, making us writhe as he does, that *this* is what he is thinking of, and *that* is what he might have been thinking of (3:174, chap. 64). Now if this account of Lydgate's beginnings had come first, its indelible effect would have made the subsequent accounts of Rosamond's campaign and conquest, if not incredible, certainly almost unbearable.

Seeing him first with Rosamond and Bulstrode convincingly introduces us to his mixed character so that the subsequent flashback bolsters our belief in his fine qualities and his potential, while enabling us still to anticipate his errors and sustain them without either contempt for him or rebellion at his fate.

The placement of a flashback for rhetorical effect may require a particular manner of narration. After Lydgate's medical excellence has been firmly established in our favoring consciousness, his folly over Laure is told by direct, omniscient narration (1:228-32, chap. 15). At this point Lydgate has no reason to rehearse this event mentally; later, when he has, the account would break the current of a highly charged scene with Rosamond (3:90, chap. 58). And the early report from the tolerant narrator prepares the reader for sympathy and the pain of watching the expected occur.

By contrast, Bulstrode's past is withheld until we have fully seen him as Middlemarch sees him, and indeed, as he sees himself. When he is forced to remember his past, it is revealed through his own mental processes and terminology, with just enough infusion by the narrator to make her judgment clear. Bulstrode had been a ''confidential accountant'' for a pawnbroker who received ''any goods offered''; he is now a ''partner in trading concerns, in which his ability was directed to economy in the raw material''; the narrative voice adds the qualification ''as in the case of the dyes which rotted Mr Vincy's silk'' (3:127-31, chap. 61). It is impossible, even in all this account of lying, swindling, and greed, not to feel something of Bulstrode's ''innocence'' as he feels it, not to compassionate his inner torment. But this sympathy would have been lost had the facts come ''straight'' from the omniscient narrator or belatedly from Bambridge at the Green Dragon or Mrs. Dollop in Slaughter Lane.

George Eliot reinforces her larger structural effects by smaller devices. One is the pairing of many characters: Dorothea and Lydgate in unhappy marriages, Casaubon and Rosamond as the ill-chosen mates; Casaubon and Lydgate in their variant aims and methods for research and their common view of a wife as an obedient admirer; Dorothea and Rosamond, Rosamond and Mrs. Garth or Mrs. Bulstrode in their responses to their husbands' efforts and failures; Dorothea and Rosamond, also Dorothea and Casaubon, in their choice of marriage for personal gratification and expansion; Rosamond and Mary Garth in their moral character and influence on their lovers; Lydgate and Mr. Garth in ambition to do good, lasting work; Lydgate and Bulstrode in their views on using people as instruments. Such a list—and it could be extended—may suggest that *Middlemarch* is full of crafty gimmicks and strained patterning. But diffused throughout the novel, these correspondences serve to link the plot lines and keep our consciousness and interest moving from one line to another. They strengthen the novel's unity by making the theme seem universally applicable. They give the sense of a thick and enmeshing social medium that pressures many characters in similar ways. Each character in a pair, by force of similarity or contrast, adds to our understanding of both and affects our distance from the other.

The pairings are especially effective for distancing when in combination with the structural device of juxtaposition. At the end of Chapter 57, Mary Garth refuses her chance to rise to "new dignities and an acknowledged value" (3:71) by destroying Fred's hopes; in Chapter 58 Rosamond begins her conscious and systematic thwarting of Lydgate's hopes and wishes in order to gain an elevated position. Again, Rosamond's unloving and untrusting response to the scandal about her innocent husband (chap. 75) is placed directly between Mrs. Bulstrode's loving fidelity to her guilty husband (chap. 74) and Dorothea's assertion of confidence in Lydgate (chap. 76), a sequence that greatly intensifies pity for Lydgate and places Rosamond at a distance from which, ironically, only Lydgate's own compassion and Dorothea's zeal can bring her back. These potent juxtapositions are employed, it is worth noting, chiefly in Lydgate's story, and they partly explain the greater sympathetic pain we feel for his misery than for Dorothea's.

By elaboration and condensation, by alternations, pairings, juxtapositions, and time reversal, George Eliot tried to place and develop the characters of *Middlemarch* so that each would have due importance and interest in her plan of plots and subplot. With so complex a scheme before her, it is a wonder that she made so few significant errors and succeeded so well, better perhaps than any other Victorian novelist attempting a similar feat.

Narration

Important as are structural placements and proportions for the rhetoric of *Middlemarch*, they depend for their maximum effect on the narrator, who binds the elements together by consistency of tone and meaning. In telling the story's events, in describing and analyzing the characters, in commenting on everything, the narrator must create the intellectual, moral, and emotional perspective that places each character at a proper distance from the reader. The narrator of *Middlemarch* is George Eliot's best; she has the deepest knowledge of and most appropriate relation to the characters (except, again, Dorothea and Will), and also the most balanced relation to the mock-reader.[13]

This narrator knows and carefully represents the internal differences between characters superficially much alike. Sidney Colvin thought that Fred and Rosamond Vincy were so much alike that George Eliot was unfair in treating the brother kindly and the sister harshly.[14] That *Middlemarch*'s best reviewer should have seen this distinction as a blot is odd, but it indicates the need, in this maze of similarities and subtle differences, for a strong narrative guide. The essential similarity of the Vincys is their egoism; the essential difference is that Fred is educable. The narrator reveals the difference through tone:

> She judged of her own symptoms as those of awakening love, and she held it still more natural that Mr Lydgate should have fallen in love at first sight of her. These things happened so often at balls, and why not by the morning light, when the

complexion showed all the better for it? Rosamond . . . was
rather used to being fallen in love with . . . had remained indif-
ferent and fastidiously critical towards both fresh sprig and fad-
ed bachelor. And here was Mr Lydgate suddenly corresponding to her ideal, being altogether foreign to Middlemarch, carrying a certain air of distinction congruous with good family,
and possessing connections which offered vistas of that middle-
class heaven, rank: a man of talent, also, whom it would be
especially delightful to enslave. (1:177, chap. 12)

Fred had . . . ample funds at disposal in his own hopefulness.
You will hardly demand that his confidence should have a basis
in external facts; such confidence, we know, is something less
coarse and materialistic: it is a comfortable disposition leading
us to expect that the wisdom of providence or the folly of our
friends, the mysteries of luck or the still greater mystery of our
high individual value in the universe, will bring about
agreeable issues, such as are consistent with our good taste in
costume, and our general preference for the best style of thing.
Fred felt sure that he should have a present from his uncle, that
he should have a run of luck, that by dint of "swapping" he
should gradually metamorphose a horse worth forty pounds into a horse that would fetch a hundred at any moment. (1:350,
chap. 23)

The passage on Rosamond is threaded with irony, but is as
humorless as her view of herself. The difference of the narrator's
judgment from Rosamond's is implied in diction that is as much
interpretive as descriptive: "fastidiously critical" is a narrative
critique of Rosamond's personality; "middle-class heaven," of
her values. The passage on Fred is ironic also, but lighthearted as
his own view of his position; its combination of elevated
phraseology, understatement, and slang points up the incongruity
of his expectations but makes them seem comical rather than
dangerous. The Rosamond passage indicates her habitual self-
absorption and suggests that anyone approaching her risks his
freedom, while the tone of the Fred passage suggests that we need
not keep him at a great emotional distance since he will harm no
one irreparably.

The characters in *Middlemarch* who most challenge our sympathetic tolerance are those who egoism lies too deep for their own recognition. Those who suffer from it may recognize it but cannot fully comprehend or judge its motives. For the reader to do so, the narrator must represent the egoist's subconscious. In the lengthy analysis of Casaubon in Chapter 42, the narrator probes every intricacy of his tormented ideas about himself, Will, and Dorothea—an utterly devastating relevation that yet compels the deepest pity for his misery:

> And who, if Mr Casaubon had chosen to expound his discontents—his suspicions that he was not any longer adored without criticism—could have denied that they were founded on good reasons? On the contrary, there was a strong reason to be added, which he had not himself taken explicitly into account—namely, that he was not unmixedly adorable. He suspected this, however, as he suspected other things, without confessing it, and like the rest of us, felt how soothing it would have been to have a companion who would never find it out. . . . Mr Casaubon, we know, had a sense of rectitude and an honorable pride in satisfying the requirements of honour, which compelled him to find other reasons for his conduct than those of jealousy and vindictiveness. The way in which Mr Casaubon put the case was this: (2:221-24, chap. 42)

Then we rise to the surface of his mind for his view of Will's acts, which view has just enough plausibility to allow him to hold it without earning the reader's contempt. The whole analysis is performed from within Casaubon's mind, yet omniscience is applied because the narrator has to expose and name those elements Casaubon cannot understand, admit, or allow out of his subconscious. Because the coming acts will be so repellant, this exposition of his mind is essential to forestall disgust. So are such firm phrases as ''like the rest of us''; before our own probable subconscious, we dare not despise Casaubon.

A narrator who knows so much about characters has an evident right to judge them. In *Middlemarch* such judgments, though often explicit, do not lack subtlety and are more reliable and effective guides to response than were such statements in many parts of the earlier novels. Sometimes actions are interpreted by a frank statement of what ought to have been done: Mr. Vincy ought to have taken "the only decisive line of conduct in relation to his daughter's engagement—namely, to inquire thoroughly into Lydgate's circumstances, declare his own inability to furnish money, and forbid alike either a speedy marriage or an engagement which must be too lengthy" (2:109, chap. 36). Likewise, Lydgate "generously but mistakenly" avoided telling Rosamond of their debts during her pregnancy (3:81, chap. 58). Both men have failed Rosamond by not involving her responsibly in the facts of her own future. They have also prevented her one possible mode of education, by small and not too painful disappointments. Later, when she is unable to rise to overwhelming demands, our memory of these narrative judgments on the two men mitigates the blame we cast on her.

Another important use of narrative interpretation is to forestall misunderstanding that would create an undesired response. Just before Rosamond begins displaying to Lydgate an active and deceptive solicitude for her mother, the narrator presents the parable of the pier glass and candle, notifying us that Rosamond will merely use her mother for her own egoistic goal (1:403, chap. 27). Our response to Rosamond must not undergo confusion or reversal. When Will wants to tell Dorothea that Casaubon "had never done more than pay a debt towards him," the narrator comments, "Will was much too good a fellow to be easy under the sense of being ungrateful. And when gratitude has become a matter of reasoning there are many ways of escaping from its bonds" (2:141, chap. 37). In other words, Will is wrong to put Casaubon's support on a basis of mere duty; Casaubon *was* generous, and we are to give him the benefit of that fact. Like Rosamond, he needs all our favor he can salvage.

Events in this novel are interpreted not only by their own context but in wider comparisons that increase our sense of the narrator's knowledge and reliability. The comparison may be with the reader's assumed experience:

Many of us looking back through life would say that the

kindest man we have ever known has been a medical man, or
perhaps that surgeon whose fine tact, directed by deeply-
informed perception, has come to us in our need with a more
sublime beneficence than that of miracle-workers. Some of
that twice-blessed mercy was always with Lydgate in his work
at the Hospital or in private houses, serving better than any
opiate to quiet and sustain him under his anxieties and his
sense of mental degeneracy. (3:206-7, chap. 66)

By its invitation to associate Lydgate with a memory of actual
kindness and knowledge, by its implication that he is equal to the
finest example we can recall, by its heightened diction and the
allusions to Scripture and Shakespeare (also part of the experience
of the cultured mock-reader), this passage greatly elevates
Lydgate in our estimation and our sympathy at the time of his
deepest decline in happiness and personal control of his fortunes.

The interpretive comparison may extend to the total world context known to this authoritative narrator and, presumably, to the
reader. When Dorothea reacts to Roman scenes as an ''oppressive masquerade of ages,'' the narrator comments:

To those who have looked at Rome with the quickening power
of a knowledge which breathes a growing soul into all historic
shapes, and traces out the suppressed transitions which unite
all contrasts, Rome may still be the spiritual centre and interpreter of the world. But let them conceive one more historical
contrast: the gigantic broken revelations of that Imperial and
Papal city thrust abruptly on the notions of a girl who had been
brought up in English and Swiss Puritanism, fed on meagre
Protestant histories and on art chiefly of the hand-screen sort.
(1:295-96, chap. 20)

The length and periodic structure of the first sentence and the
wide allusions to Roman history lend dignity and authority to the
narrative voice, while ''notions of a girl,'' ''meagre Protestant
histories,'' and ''the hand-screen sort'' enforce the contrast that
is crushing Dorothea. Thus her suffering is dignified to a level
worthy of more understanding and compassion than the nervous
tears of an excitable girl.

Finally, the context for interpretation may extend to universal human tendencies: "He was simply a man whose desires had been stronger than his theoretic beliefs, and who had gradually explained the gratification of his desires into satisfactory agreement with those beliefs. If this be hypocrisy, it is a process which shows itself occasionally in us all . . ." (3:132, chap. 61). This cuts into every reader's subconscious as well as Bulstrode's; the narrator even includes herself and the whole human race in the indictment, thus requiring of the reader a sense of total human solidarity that will encompass all the world's Bulstrodes, in or out of novels. This sense of solidarity, this union of art and life, was George Eliot's ultimate rhetorical aim. In this case, it may be just to say that any failure to achieve it must be the result of a deficiency in the receptive apparatus of the real reader.

All the techniques of interpretation just noted have presupposed not only the narrator's total knowledge of the characters but her cordial respect for the reader. If we review *Adam Bede* for some of the unfavorable assumptions, reproofs, lectures, and explanations of the obvious that are offered the reader, it is immediately evident how much more sophisticated is the relation of *Middlemarch's* narrator to the mock-reader. Though there are still many ironic reminders of our likenesses to the Middlemarchers and of our need to correct our views, the old "I-you" opposition is virtually gone. "You" becomes "anyone" or expands into a genuine "we" that binds narrator and reader in a shared knowledge and opinion and in a sympathy for even the least lovable characters in our common human lot of dim vision and much disappointment.

It is noticeable that the narrative techniques just discussed are used rather freely for most characters but must be hunted in the presentations of Dorothea and Will. In their dramatic scenes together, the narrator records their thoughts and feelings but supplies little or no narrative analysis of their subconscious motives, and no clear interpretation of their wisdom or folly about each other. In the nondramatic descriptions and analyses of their separate thoughts and reactions, they are seldom linked to the histories of real people, but often to those in fairy tales and myths:

Dorothea is like "a princess in the days of enchantment" who sees a "four-footed creature . . .with a human gaze" full of "choice and beseeching" (3:9, chap. 54). Generalized pronouns and comments are extremely scarce. These facts create the impression, not that this love is uniquely beautiful, but rather that it is simply incredible, at least as interpreted. Interpretation is, of course, implied in these nondramatic analyses, but it is often contradictory or ambiguous.

The ambiguity is the result of the dichotomy within Dorothea's and Will's illustrative functions—the idealized and glorified Platonic lovers versus the mates in a sadly unequal match. The narrator cannot have the interpretation both ways and cannot make a satisfying choice. This is so severe a problem in the distancing of Will and Dorothea, and it so blurs the pattern of her career, that it must be discussed separately at some length in relation to their total characterization. Here we may note that the narrator, in what seems a desperate effort to compensate for failure to realize her characters coherently within the story, presses a rhetoric outside it by means of the Prelude and the epigraphs of chapters.

Epigraphs and Prelude are designed, it seems, to dictate the glorification of the lovers; and the epigraphs do consistently exalt Dorothea's virtues (even her faults) and Ladislaw's virtue and happiness in loving her. Often an epigraph offers a laudatory interpretation that is contradicted by the rather ludicrous representation within the chapter. Chapter 47, for instance, has an epigraph about the "truest love" that is "highest gain" and that springs as naturally as flowers; but it shows Will first thinking of his love in the inflated language of sonnets and medieval romances, and then, having "silenced Objection by force of unreason," going to Lowick church to glimpse his lady and coming away feeling "utterly ridiculous, out of temper, and miserable." Even in the epigraphs, however, one occasionally wonders if the narrator is pressing a satiric irony. Dante may have been serious in idealizing the gentle lady and the pale, trembling, but blessed lover of *La Vita Nuova*, but by the Victorian age, a more comic eye was cast upon courtly love. When the narrator, then, quotes Dante in the epigraph of Chapter 54, is she of his mind or her own age's?

The Prelude definitely epitomizes the ambiguity that pervades the novel. In it the narrator opens all the stops in glorifying Dorothea and demanding compassionate admiration for her Theresa-like "flame," her "spiritual grandeur ill-matched with the meanness of opportunity," her "ardently willing soul," her "loving heart-beats and sobs after an unattained goodness." This is really dreadful writing and dreadful pressure on the reader, and by its prefatory position the passage sets up an expectation and requirement that no amount of rhetoric through realistic characterization could possibly achieve. But the Prelude also declares that Dorothea, this wondrous ideal woman, had a "life of mistakes . . . *perhaps* a tragic failure. . . ." Her struggles "to common eyes . . . *seemed* mere inconsistency and formlessness," so that her choice of "a vague ideal" (lamp-holder to Casaubon) was "disapproved as extravagance" and her choice of "the common yearning of womanhood" (marriage for love of Will) was "condemned as a lapse" (italics added). Well then, *is* Dorothea's life a tragic failure? *Is* the marriage to Will one of her mistakes? Is it a lapse? If we say Yes, are we "common minds" or at one with the narrator in recognizing the truth? If the marriage is not a mistake or a lapse, how can Dorothea be tragic or even gravely diminished? And if it is, how can she be so glorious? The confusion is found even in the Prelude and is certainly continued within the story.

When the narrator of *Middlemarch* knows her characters truly and presents them consistently, she is superb in controlling all relations among characters, reader, and herself. But when she deals with Dorothea and the one man who offers her the total love and appreciation that the narrator believes she deserves, then the narrator herself becomes one of the most myopic, almost maudlin characters George Eliot ever created. Such an inconsistency boggles the critical mind.

The Tragic Plots—Rhetoric of Character and Event

Despite George Eliot's general success with the rhetoric of structure and narration in *Middlemarch*, we must still question how successfully she portrays and distances Dorothea and Lydgate as protagonists in parallel tragedies of uncommon potential stultified in a commonplace society.

Their cases are initially similar. Both have high levels of intelligence, social awareness, and concern, and a will to do good for others. Both have some possibility of actually doing good if they choose and act carefully in their particular circumstances, though Dorothea, as a woman in Victorian society, is much more limited and can hardly hope to have her epic life except through marriage. Both fail because of inherent character defects and social influences that lead them into marriages that are disastrous to their personal happiness and social aspirations. It seems clear that both are meant to move us with tragic or near-tragic emotion all the way.

But there the similarities end. Dorothea is allowed to escape her oppressive marriage and to enter another which, if not clearly and totally fulfilling, is certainly not tragically destructive. Lydgate remains a ''noble mind o'erthrown'' by the ''spots of commonness'' that enslaved him to his worthless wife. Dorothea's story, initially clear enough in its pattern and rhetoric (clear within the story, not in the Prelude), becomes confused and ambiguous. Lydgate's story remains an almost fully sucessful tragedy. The difference is due to the rhetoric of character and event, supported—or confused—by narrative style.

If Dorothea is to be experienced as a ''tragic failure'' or even as seriously diminished, then her rhetorical treatment must truthfully reveal her potential and her weakness and must establish a congruity in our responses to both the marriages by which she seeks and loses her fulfillment. The first marriage would be indeed a disaster if it lasted; since it does not, it need cause only a limited distress, can even carry a degree of humor. But a second and lasting error should absolutely make us weep. It is evident that we do experience the Casaubon marriage for what it is, but the Ladislaw marriage makes us weep mainly because we cannot be sure that we are meant to do so.

The general rhetorical clarity about the first marriage is owing to two factors: the narrator's clarity and control, and effective use of character interaction. As a preparation for Dorothea's rapid and foolish decision, the narrator presents her character quickly and directly. She describes her from outside and in, mixing Dorothea's ideas and diction with her own to suggest the appropriate response:

> [To Dorothea] the destinies of mankind, seen by the light of Christianity, made the *solicitudes* of feminine fashion appear an occupation for *Bedlam*. She could not reconcile the *anxieties* of a spiritual life involving eternal consequences, with a keen interest in guimp and artificial protrusions of drapery. Her mind was *theoretic*, and yearned by its nature after some *lofty conception* of the world which might frankly include the parish of Tipton and her own rule of conduct there; she was *enamoured* of intensity and greatness, and *rash* in *embracing* whatever seemed to her to have those aspects; likely to seek martyrdom, to make retractations, and then to incur martyrdom after all in a quarter where she had not sought it. Certainly such elements in the character of a marriageable girl tended to interfere with her lot, and hinder it from being decided according to custom, by good looks, vanity, and merely canine affection. (1:8-9, chap. 1; italics added)

The italicized words all connote some extremity of response appropriate only to momentous affairs, not to a habitual outlook on daily business. They describe Dorothea's own attitudes and her judgments of others' attitudes, but they are not really words she would use to describe herself; certainly she does not think herself ''rash.'' The narrator, therefore, who chose the words, is distanced from her by knowledge of her weakness. But the narrator also knows the attitudes of the surrounding society, which expects of a woman a little religious sentiment, a lot of interest in clothing, and a marriage decided by physical and materialistic considerations. Dorothea's resistance to such norms is a virtue, and her "martyrdom" will be pitiable; the tone of benevolent humor suggests, however, that it will not ultimately be tragic unless she persists in her rashness. The excess in the narrator's admiration is revealed only in the rather shrewish "canine affection," which is unfair, in advance, to Sir James. (A similar narrative bias is shown elsewhere in these early chapters by some heavy irony and loaded diction: "the pathetic loveliness of all spontaneous trust" (1:38, chap. 3). But the fault is not frequent in this section.) The narrated representation is supported by Dorothea's interaction with Celia, which places Dorothea's histrionics against her sister's shrewd observation and common sense. This juxtaposition with Celia continues in smaller ways in the ensuing chapters, where the narrator bolsters Dorothea by using diminishing analogies for Celia (cherub, squirrel, Murr the Cat), and where dialogue reveals their differences in speech and tastes and levels of self-assurance. Better to be foolish and fine-minded than wordly-wise and light-minded. Dorothea, at least, is that rare egoist who has some humility. So if her idealism leads her to misery, she will be pitiable rather than contemptible.

During Casaubon's courtship (chaps. 2 through 10), the clear rhetorical purpose is so to reveal the couple as to win informed sympathy for their mutual error, with the greater share of the sympathy prepared for Dorothea. The technique used is a rhetoric of juxtaposed characters, with the narrator present to give what additional guidance is needed.

In chapters 2 through 6, the dominant view is Dorothea's of Casaubon, presented with a blend of compassion and comic irony that spares us the sick foreboding with which we watch Lydgate sucked into the vortex. The blend arises from a folding of Casaubon's and the narrator's own views into Dorothea's:

> What delightful companionship! Mr Casaubon seemed even unconscious that trivialities existed, and never handed round that small-talk of heavy men. . . . He talked of what he was interested in, or else he was silent and bowed with sad civility. To Dorothea, this was adorable genuineness, and religious abstinence from that artificiality which uses up the soul in the

efforts of pretence. . . . He assented to her expressions of
devout feeling, and usually with an appropriate
quotation. . . . Mr Casaubon apparently did not care about
building cottages, and diverted the talk to the extremely narrow accommodation which was to be had in the dwellings of
the ancient Egyptians. . . . But further reflection told her that
she was presumptuous in demanding his attention to such a
subject. (1:46-47, chap. 3)

The diction describing Casaubon is drawn from Dorothea's viewpoint and from earlier descriptions of *her* own mind that she is
thus imposing on him; but through her myopia come some of
Casaubon's own stuffy diction and the narrator's true vision of
Casaubon's egocentricity; he is not to the narrator (or reader) as
he is "to Dorothea." Yet since we have heard the "small talk"
of Sir James and Mr. Brooke, we are compelled to understand and
pity Dorothea's mistake. And the humor assures us that the marriage will be a severe checkmate but not an irreparable disaster.

In Chapters 7 through 9, Dorothea and Casaubon are each
judged by Celia, Mr. Brooke, Sir James, the Cadwalladers, and
Will. Their views are presented in dramatic dialogues or personal
reflections, which generally are allowed to stand without admix-
ture of the narrator's diction. Either they are clearly correct or
their limits are clear. All these characters influence the reader's
views of Dorothea and Casaubon, but none is sufficiently informed
about either to be a fully reliable judge. The narrator at length
refers specifically to their biases and turns to examine Casaubon's
own views (1:125-28, chap. 10).

This passage is the first major view into Casaubon's mind, and
the diction tells of "hindrances," "fading of hopes," "fixity of
self-delusion," "loneliness," "despair," "weary experience,"
"blankness of sensibility," and "universal pressure, which will
one day be too heavy for him." Such accumulated negative
descriptions of his habitual life compel us to sympathize with his
hope of alleviating sadness by marriage and, with the narrator, to
"feel more tenderly toward his experience of success" that
brings no joy.

This passage prepares us for the change of tone after the marriage, a change that is appropriate because the union is now a serious, painful affair for both partners. The narrator maintains distance by a firm fairness to both. Dorothea's need to feel her husband's suffering is exhibited as much as her pain from his deficiencies.[15] In Dorothea's case, the small reminder of narrative irony ("But was not Mr. Casaubon as learned as before? . . . O waywardness of womanhood! [1:298, chap. 20]) changes quickly to a tone of compassion for a girl suffering what she cannot understand. The narrator does understand and offers explanations that prevent our reacting to her misery as Mrs. Cadwallader might, with satiric satisfaction in our own prophetic souls. As soon as Casaubon begins to suffer from Dorothea, the narrative tone shifts from mocking irony to pity to analytic firmness. Analyses of him are timed to coincide nearly with the same revelation to Dorothea, so that we may sympathize with her struggle to comprehend him, yet keep ahead of her. This educative process of both reader and Dorothea culminates at the end of Chapter 42 with her movement out of lingering egoism into a true sense of his separate needs and pains, and with his one genuine moment of altruistic response. At this point, the narrator's, reader's, and Dorothea's awareness and judgment coincide.

Unfortunately, the marriage does not end with this moment of reconciliation and George Eliot subsequently raised and left unresolved the thorny question of Dorothea's decision to accede to Casaubon's demand for posthumous control of her life. Is this decision heroic charity on her part? Or is it a sign of her lingering immaturity, of inability to assert her individual freedom? The narrator does indeed supply all the pros and cons of the question, but solely as they struggle through Dorothea's tortured mind (2:311-14, chap. 48). No judgment is passed or even implied by commentary, style, or the working out of the action. We are told: "She saw clearly enough the whole situation, yet she was fettered: she could not smite the stricken soul that entreated hers. If that were weakness, Dorothea was weak" (2:317, chap. 48).

But *is* it weakness, in the narrator's view? Later we are told that, bound by her pledge, Dorothea would have been capable of a task she knew to be vain "for all uses except that consecration of faithfulness which is a supreme use" (2:335, chap. 50). The last clause seems to express the narrator's evaluation as much as Dorothea's. If, then, the work would have had that value, why is Dorothea allowed to escape by so obviously contrived an event as her husband's death at just the crucial moment? The contrivance looks suspiciously like George Eliot's inability to deny Dorothea either her heroic act or Will Ladislaw. She must be glorified for her "compassion" and her submission to "the ideal and not the real yoke of marriage." But she must also be delivered from an error that is so largely her society's fault and be rewarded for her self-sacrifice; and she must become the heroic lover of the one man who ideally loves her. Thus the confusion that will pervade the depiction of the Will-Dorothea relationship has seeped heavily into the last of the Casaubon relation; two deeds for which Dorothea is to be glorified cannot be reconciled to each other.

Furthermore, glorifying her submission and then letting her escape it conflicts with her role as tragic victim of her unwise choices; and of course the glorification is incongruous with the represented fact that she *is* weak in submitting to an irrational demand and is compulsive to the point of self-deception. George Eliot seems to attempt a retrieval of this error of Dorothea's character by her subsequent rejection of the Synoptical Tabulation with the note that she could not submit her soul; but even this act is rhetorically ambiguous. Are we to respond to it as a new, sane realism or as a posthumous striking of Casaubon's soul?[16]

Except in its conclusion, Dorothea's first marriage is both represented and interpreted with firm and consistent rhetoric. Casaubon's character is always clear; so is Dorothea's relation to him. We know the reason for her error and are inevitably relieved by her (and his) deliverance. Afterward it is clear that she has new maturity and new resources for the exercise of her intelligence and unselfish ardor.

It is also clear that she will eventually marry Will Ladislaw. Because all events in Dorothea's story so far have suggested that she is parallel to Lydgate in being an uncommon person tragically or seriously diminished in an unsatisfactory marriage, the reader has, at this point, a reasonable expectation that her new marriage will be clearly treated as a second, even more pitiable error and source of dissatisfaction for her. Or, if it is to be a happy, mainly satisfying affair to Dorothea's perception, then she must be seen as finally diminished and deceived, which also would be at least pathetic if not tragic. But if the reader too is to be happy and satisfied for her, then Dorothea is no longer parallel to Lydgate but to Fred Vincy; her role in the plot has been changed—a switch that no rhetoric can justify or make acceptable. The fact is that all three interpretations pertain to some extent, and the result is rhetorical chaos and the loss of any sense of tragedy in Dorothea's story. The source of the trouble is the rhetorically flawed characterization of Will and hence of Dorothea as his lover.[17]

Without a clear portrayal of Will, we cannot know whether he is seriously and permanently inadequate for Dorothea, inadequate but partially redeemed by his genuine love for her, or a good mentor and wonderfully loving mate for a redeemed idealist like her (interpretations roughly corresponding to the three versions of the marriage). As an individual, is Will an amusing dilettante and romantic, or another idealized soul, unjustly depreciated by a crass society? If the former, does he mature enough to warrant his success in love and marriage? Critics may decide, but the novel never does.

The ambiguity flows first from Will's representation as a masculine adult. Physical description runs constantly in terms of light, bright curls (which he constantly shakes), delicate rippling nose, delicate throat, delicate petulant profile, transparent, even translucent skin (he has much "inward light"), and an expression of pouting or discontent. Nor are these details always the critical vision of the town or the idealizing vision of Dorothea. To contrast Will with Casaubon, we are told:

> Surely, his very features changed their form; his jaw looked sometimes large and sometimes small; and the little ripple in his nose was a preparation for metamorphosis. When he turned his head quickly his hair seemed to shake out light, and some persons thought they saw decided genius in this coruscation. (1:321, chap. 21)

The reader is dissociated from "some persons," and the "Surely" may be ironic mockery, as may the suggestion of the sun-god. Yet—does not the passage suggest some special brilliance and charm about Will? It has been called the "author's parody of Dorothea's view,"[18] which is apt, but the narrator is still in it.

It is the narrator who presents the mythological analogies: Ariel, the incarnation of the spring, and the spirit of morning—all more distancing than humanizing in their effect on Will's representation. Dorothea, the narrator says, "did not know then that it was Love who had come to her . . . with the hues of morning on his wings—that it was Love to whom she was sobbing her farewell as his image was banished. . . ." (3:22, chap. 55). Granted, the allusion is to Cupid, but Dorothea has just said good-bye to Will, whose identity the narrator does know, whom she thus idealizes without a trace of irony.

Even more ambiguous than Will's masculinity is his personal character and potential. Before the death of Casaubon, the image of the dilettante prevails and is the butt of plentiful irony. The long opening of Chapter 10 describes Will awaiting "messages from the universe" to his "genius"; satire flows from the combination of inflated diction, understatement of his foolish actions, and the mocking tone of narrative voice. Yet even here, by contrast to Casaubon, a doubt is introduced whether Will's potential is negated by the irony or is to be taken seriously, as merely needing realistic circumstances.

The rhetoric of interplay of character suggests no very serious view of Will. In Rome, Naumann shows him up as a Romantic idler and occasional worker; even Dorothea notes that poems would be required of his poetic soul (1:342, chap. 22). At home he is deflated by Brooke's patronage, inane praises, and persistent comparisons to major poets and politicians. To Mrs. Cadwallader he is a Byronic hero, a pretty but dangerous sprig. We are accustomed to keen perception from Mrs. Cadwallader; are we to judge Will as lightly as she does or to assume that he has a worth all these narrow and conventional people cannot see? Farebrother and Lydgate are the only sensible people who like him, and they do not take him very seriously. Indeed, he suffers severely by contrast with Lydgate, who has a defined and worthy goal for work.

Just before the death of Casaubon, the narrator makes a thoroughly satiric summary of Will's condition: but for his desire to be near Dorothea, he would have been in Italy starting and stopping dramas, prose, verses, and copies of paintings. For lack of better occupation in Middlemarch, he has "accepted his bit of work" in politics (3:285, chap. 46). It would seem, then, that Will Ladislaw is satirized as an amateur and that he was created to satirize others even more ridiculous and unproductive than he. In Lydgate's phrase, he is "miscellaneous and *bric-à-brac*, but likable" (2:247, chap. 43).

Dorothea, of course, loves, not likes, Will; and he must function primarily as her lover. If he is to be solely a Platonic lover, romanticizing his love for her like his love for art, then the satiric interpretation is appropriate and should remain clear and steady. Looking at Will as lover, again up to the death of Casaubon, we do see the same dominant satiric treatment, but marked with even more ambiguity. Interior views show him as a courtly lover, full of passionate and puerile adoration and jealousy (1:333-34, chap. 22). His "choric wail" over the "most horrible of virgin-sacrifices" and his resolution to watch over Dorothea like a guardian slave are counterpointed by the narrator's "simple truth" that her presence enticed him strongly (2:132-33, chap. 37). But, on almost the next pages, when he succeeds in seeing her, we are told that his feelings then "were perfect, for we mortals have our divine moments" (2:136-37). When Will reacts to Dorothea's entrance as to "effective magic" or "joy in the morning light over . . . white mountain top" (2:173, chap. 39), the diction suggests vague, esoteric passion, but there is no sure irony in the passage. When the narrator describes them as "like two fond children who were talking confidentially of birds" (2:180, chap. 39), is that meant to be deflating? Or are we to admire their sexual innocence (naiveté)? Are we meant to share Will's persistent view of his experience as a verification of "higher love poetry" (2:298, chap. 47)?

Thus, during Casaubon's life, ambiguity clings like a wet cloth to the portrait of Will the hopeless lover. He cannot be wholly childish or ridiculous, because he loves Dorothea, the lovely, suffering heroine, as she deserves to be loved. But an equally strong view is that his love is romanticism, without a solid base in either his own character or his knowledge of Dorothea, both required if his marriage is to be even as satisfactory as Fred Vincy's.

If Will is to be Dorothea's second mistake, he can remain immature both as man and lover; he will then fit the requirement of the tragic plot. But if he is to be viewed positively, let alone glorified for his love, if we are to be at all satisfied to have him marry Dorothea, then represented facts must show a genuine maturation in him, and the narrator's irony should alter to fit the facts. After Casaubon's death, when Will decides to leave Middlemarch, he is still in a "dream of wonders that he might do . . . . probable enough in the inward order of things" (2:356-57, chap. 51). No evidence is offered that he accomplishes much during his absence, and his resolution to stay away is lightly, negatively described as "simply a state of mind liable to melt into a minuet with other states of mind, and to find itself bowing, smiling, and giving place with polite facility" (3:410, chap. 82).

The narrator's attitude of critical amusement apparently has not changed. Yet when Dorothea, in the very next chapter, pledges herself to marry this man, the narrator seems unconscious of a problem. The whole scene is done exclusively from their viewpoints, without interpretation. Will says he will probably be "a mere pen and a mouthpiece"; neither he nor the narrator suggests that he would work to be something better for Dorothea's sake (3:426, chap. 83). Later we are told that he did eventually work well as a public man, but that reform did not

amount to much. Dorothea, then, has made herself a helpmate to
a very middling sort of man. Is that a tragedy for her, or not?

Perhaps we are to believe that the matured depth of his love
will compensate for his personal inadequacies? His late view of
their love is in terms of a "world apart, where the sunshine fell
on tall white lilies" (3:415, chap. 82)—no narrative comment. In
their final scene, he is moved to a "sob" at her statement of faith
in him; the narrative tone is serious-pathetic. But the next
sentence is comic-ironic; he "might have done for the portrait of
a Royalist" (3:422, chap. 83). From beginning to end, ambiguity
and unsteadiness mark the narrative treatment of Will's idealization of Dorothea, making it seem, now the product of his volatile
nature and inflated self-image, and now the manifestation of the
finest, truest part of his character, which vibrates to the finest and
least appreciated parts of hers.

In sum, Will is represented mimetically almost all one way, as
an occupational amateur and an ordinary man with a normal sexual love who romanticizes it into courtly love. But he is interpreted two ways—one as represented, the other as a noble Dante
figure, who alone properly worships the perfect Victorian
Beatrice.

And what of the lady? About Dorothea's noble character the
narrator is never in doubt; but she does portray her view of Will
with nearly the same ambiguity as clouds his view of her.
Dorothea idealizes Will beyond our power to sympathize and
almost beyond our power to excuse her. Yet the narrator seldom
offers rhetorical guidance as to which we should do. To the death
of Casaubon, Dorothea's love for Will is clearly a compensation
for her need to have "young companionship" and "to rule
beneficently" (2:133-34, chap. 37). Yet she wants to rule "by
making the joy of another soul"; that, presumably is a worthy
sentiment. Then is "Poor Dorothea" to be pitied because she is
now overestimating Will as she once did Casaubon or because she
is not free to enjoy his really worthwhile conversation and admiration? Is her second error being prepared and explained, or
her real and satisfying love and marriage? The reader must guess.

There is no doubt her sexless response betrays naiveté about the dynamics of her situation.[19] But now no narrative irony touches her blindness, as it did touch her blindness about Casaubon. She is an ''unhappy child'' to be pitied and very seldom laughed at; that bespeaks her immaturity. But she is also an ''ardent woman'' whose love is the sign of her poetic spirit and pure mind.

After the death of Casaubon, we have a variable rhetoric of character to guide our responses to Dorothea as a woman and as Will's lover. Shrewd Mrs. Cadwallader warns her against ''playing tragedy queen and taking things sublimely,'' and she warns her husband that Dorothea will make the usual ''woman's choice . . . taking the only man she can get'' (3:6-8, chap. 54). That certainly carries Mrs. Cadwallader's usual sting of truth and therefore carries rhetorical conviction; but she and all the others at Tipton and Freshitt are at least partially wrong about Ladislaw's motives, and Dorothea alone is right. The honor due Dorothea for that faith is validated by her subsequent correct judgment of Lydgate in his worst circumstances. Lydgate, in his response to her trust, offers a romanticized view of her as a ''Virgin Mary'' gazing down ''at the poor mortals who pray to her''; but he also perceives her propensity to ''heroic hallucination'' and wonders about her ''unusual feeling'' for Ladislaw without, however, making any judgment upon it (3:361-62, chap. 76). The narrator makes no comment on Lydgate's musings; but elsewhere she treats Dorothea's response to the misjudgments of both men as an unequivocal sign of her nobility of mind and her forever ''ardent'' spirit and ''yearning'' to right wrongs and do ''some active good.''

The narrator's treatment of Dorothea's love in the last half of the novel offers the oddest mixture of pathos, condescension as to a child, and admiration for her unsullied passion. The two parting scenes are rendered in diction of sobs, throbs, and tremors—Dorothea's emotion without implied comment. After the first parting, the narrator warns against reproach of her fine feelings, but also links her grief to that of children and Dorothea herself to "ardent souls . . . apt to commit themselves to the fulfillment of their own wishes" (3:22-23, chap. 55). This sounds as if she will repeat her error with Casaubon. During her night of grief (chap. 80), however, she comes to a fairly mature recognition of her passion, not for a "bright creature" but a "living man." We are clearly meant to admire the heroism with which she conquers her jealousy and returns to Rosamond. But two days later, she is reduced to the ludicrous by her efforts to study the geography of Asia Minor; the narrative irony is precisely that of Chapters 1 through 10. And the final scene again represents her and Will as "two children looking out on the storm" (3:424, chap. 85). We cannot respond to her love as equally noble and childish. And the Finale tells nothing of its postmarital development, only that it remained stronger than her feeling that there was "something better which she might have done." She is still dissatisfied with her sphere of activity, but not with her husband.

If Dorothea, then, has accommodated to a lowered ideal of life, how does this affect our final estimate of her? She certainly has not the pathos of Lydgate, but does she even convince us of a potential for wide good that could have been realized in other circumstances? At the end she still feels the need to have "been better and known better," and she is satisfied to give "wifely help" in "beneficent activity which she had not the doubtful pains of discovering . . . for herself" (3:461, finale). She sounds in much the same mental state as at the beginning of the novel. Yet the narrator ends with a reassertion that she had "noble impulse," "great feelings," and "great faith," that the "mixed results" of her life were owing to "the conditions of an imperfect social state." She is still a "new Theresa" lacking only opportunity. Thus we return to the Prelude.

But the final rhetoric cannot nullify all the dubieties about Dorothea. Supposing a different and better society, it is not clear that her noble impulses would have been any better guides or produced better results. Dorothea may be finer than anyone in her world, but her faults and her failure to be great cannot all be blamed on that world. We could accept the judgment in the epigraph of Chapter 55, that her faults are "the fruity must of soundest wine" (3:21); but without the constant pressure of honorific adjectives, we would hardly know that we are supposed to exalt those faults as virtues. And even with pressure, we cannot so respond. The facts do not always win sympathy for Dorothea when the narrator intends it, and when she intends it is not always clear.

Dorothea, then, starts out to be the protagonist of a tragedy but ceases to be that in the end. George Eliot finds her too lovable and admirable, finally, to wreck her life a second time. About Tertius Lydgate, though she regards him highly, she has no such compunction. Consequently, she was able to meet the terms of novel's subject, theme, and required rhetoric and to make of Lydgate's story her first consistent and almost wholly successful tragic plot.

To be rhetorically successful as a tragic protagonist, Lydgate must have convincing potential for greatness; his personal distinction must outweigh his character defect, which must be seen as a flaw and not as a grave and pervasive moral disorder. The flaw must not make him contemptible beyond our power to pity, but it must wreck his life with an absolutely convincing inevitability. And the rhetorical tone throughout must be firm and just, yet compassionate.

The effect of Chapter 15 in building up Lydgate as a doctor, a scientist, and a compassionate man has been previously remarked. Subsequent dramatizations of his private research and public practice reinforce this effect and raise again our admiration for him, belief in him, and desire for his success. Knowledge and sympathy make him the town's best doctor and raise him above the petty rivalry that poisons altruism in other social leaders. His ultimate failure, therefore, must be felt as the ruin of real potential for doing great good.

The personal flaws that wreck Lydgate—conceit, rashness, and, above all, his essentially vulgar but conventional view of women and of a wife's role—are all unsparingly represented. They are blended with his excellence in the descriptions of him as they are blended in his character; they are sufficiently dramatized, as in his conversations with Rosamond; and they are thoroughly analyzed and recalled by brief notations. But the total emphasis is on their proportionately minor nature—Lydgate is "a little too self-confident and disdainful . . . a little spotted with commonness . . . a little pinched here and protruberant there with native prejudices" (1:226, chap. 15); these diminutives underline the tragic irony in the total wreckage of his hopes.

The narrator's pleas that Lydgate's "little" faults should not alienate our "interest in him" would not prevent our despising him for being so easily trapped and destroyed, despite his self-assurance, were it not for the skillful portrayals of Bulstrode and Rosamond. The dialogues and events that reveal them let us pity Lydgate for their effect on him and also for his response to them.

Bulstrode in the beginning is presented as just ambiguous enough to ensnare a man of honor and ambition. Up to the Tyke affair, we know just what the Middlemarchers know of Bulstrode and almost certainly share their opinion of him. But we also see how he is like the townsmen, merely sheltering his hypocrisy behind better public intentions—the very intentions most apt to engage Lydgate. The debate and voting about Tyke (chap. 18) demonstrate Lydgate's relation to Bulstrode and the townsmen: for all their resemblance to the banker, they are more independent of him than is the self-assured and honorable doctor. The irony is pitiable.

Before the scandal breaks, however, any ambiguity about Bulstrode is removed for the reader. He knows exactly Bulstrode's motives and Lydgate's degree of culpability, and is therefore properly distanced from the town's opinions and enabled to share that sympathy for Bulstrode's disgrace by which Lydgate is ennobled in his own time of defeat. The riotous humor of the discussions at Dollop's and elsewhere sharpens the edge of pity for Bulstrode and Lydgate; their misery is everyone else's self-righteous delight. And despite Bulstrode's own self-righteousness at the Board meeting, we are compelled to side with him, as Lydgate does, against the needless cruelty of the public exposure. When Lydgate's instinct as a healer operates more strongly than personal caution and thus completes his fall in the town's eyes, it elevates him in ours. The elevation and our pity for him are confirmed by his own self-questioning and admissions to Dorothea and, above all, by his refusal to exonerate himself by aggravating the case against Bulstrode.

In relation to Bulstrode, therefore, Lydgate is seen as a man of noble dimensions but dangerous pride, understandably but tragically deceived, ensnared, and destroyed. In relation to Rosamond, Lydgate should seem not a fool but a victim of his own masculine prejudices and his emotional need and of her misshapen personality. This calls for some differences in Rosamond's delineation before and after her marriage. Before it, she must be made credibly deceptive, so that the reader can comprehend Lydgate's fall into her trap. After it, the reader, though knowing Rosamond, must be enabled to feel Lydgate's shock of discovery. And in the end, Rosamond must yield just enough to make Lydgate's final resignation seem a sadly inevitable yet morally right decision.

To make Lydgate's entrapment credible, the early representation of Rosamond stresses the externals that deceive him: her beauty, her polished manners, and especially her conversation, free from either boasting or false humility (chaps. 16, 27). Only five very short and superficial conversations occur between Lydgate and Rosamond before their marriage, and in them the brevity and conscious cleverness of her speech effectively hide her real motives.

George Eliot apparently revised the text to make Rosamond's deliberate scheming clear to the reader,[20] but it could hardly be so to Lydgate. Sometimes their two minds are juxtaposed to show the variances utterly unknown to each (chaps. 16, 27, 36); and Lydgate's mind is seen as "spotted" indeed, but of so much finer a quality that he cannot conceive what is going on in Rosamond's. She might well deceive the reader too, had he not the accompanying narration and her conversations with her mother, brother, and Mary Garth. Finally, in the engagement scene, Rosamond's "helpless quivering," her naturalness, and her loss of "self-contented grace" are made sufficiently appealing that the reader's sympathy may be caught momentarily almost like Lydgate's. He may feel only later the full irony of Lydgate's marriage beginning and climaxing in his ministration to Rosamond's pain, as if she were a patient (2:43-44, chap. 31; 3:408, chap. 81).

After the marriage, Rosamond's victimization of Lydgate requires some action independent of him and conquest of him when they clash. These must be presented so that we pity Lydgate and yet recognize his continuing responsibility for his own fall. Rosamond's secret deceptions and her pseudo-infidelity with Will impress on us Lydgate's pitiable isolation and the irony of his assumptions of his control and her docility. Their clashes are recorded in thirteen substantial dialogues that increase in frequency and level of conflict as the marriage deteriorates. They also take on a pattern: Lydgate's proposals, Rosamond's counterproposals, his alternating anger and tenderness, her rejection of him and of their problem. Their exchanges employ "we" only for the measures each wants and the other rejects; otherwise the discussion is in I-you terms; it is his problem, not hers, and he unconsciously encourages this by demanding blind obedience to what he has previously decided without consulting her. They are both in error, and we pity them both; but because Lydgate is far less selfish and more realistic and loving, and is losing far more, we pity him more.

These clashes are the only real "events" of Lydgate's marriage. Not Victorian reticence alone kept George Eliot from creating scenes of early love or intimacy. She wisely omitted any domestic or social events, which would have distracted from our sense of Lydgate's rapid and dreadful discovery, his shock, and the subsequent unremitting friction upon his spirit. He is always trapped, trapped, trapped.

Pity for Lydgate ultimately requires that Rosamond be utterly unsympathetic yet very fairly treated, and in this representation and interpretation George Eliot succeeded as never before. Rosamond's portrait is free of the animus that marred Hetty Sorrel's, probably because Lydgate is not revered quite as Adam Bede was. He deserves some retribution for his commonplace attitudes that have helped to create such women as Rosamond. But she is given what redemption her nature allows so that both Lydgate and the reader can pityingly accept her as his burden.

But it should also be clear just how far Rosamond will yield and how far, therefore, Lydgate must resign himself. Specifically, we must ask if he has to refuse Dorothea's support of the hospital. Unless the rhetoric of character and event convinces us of this, Lydgate's complete fall from his potential lacks inevitability and we cannot fully pity it. Certainly, Lydgate is discouraged, Rosamond still wants to go to London, and Dorothea is given to idealistic "plans." But Lydgate is resilient and somewhat reinspirited by Dorothea, as Rosamond is moved to unwonted goodness; and Dorothea does have ample funds to maintain an independent hospital and give Lydgate a just income for meritorious work. Further, in the scene with Rosamond (chap. 81), Dorothea seems just on the verge of pleading, with some likelihood of success, that she remain in Middlemarch, when Lydgate reenters, making what looks like an interruption authorially contrived to evade the issue of Rosamond's consent.

Nor is the narrative interpretation any real help here. In Dorothea's interviews with Lydgate (chap. 76) and with Rosamond (chap. 81), all the narration represents the three characters' thoughts and feelings. No diction or comment implies whether Lydgate is realistic and honorable in his refusal, whether he would not reverse it if Rosamond consented, or whether (as the evidence easily suggests) he is needlessly capitulating and so depriving the town of medical benefit, Dorothea of the one good she might have done, and himself of manly honor. Unless we feel sure what Lydgate could and should have done, we cannot be sure how to respond to what he does do.

This note of uncertainty is unusual in the Lydgate story, habitually so firmly conceived and executed. It almost certainly relates to ambivalence about Dorothea's sacrifice of fortune to marry Will. A commitment to the hospital would surely have secured her against this. Once again, George Eliot cannot give Dorothea both her heroic deed of generosity and her fulfillment of love and cannot sacrifice either; and once again, this dubiety invades a story that is otherwise rhetorically clear and successful. The effect on Lydgate's tragedy is to make his final misery in London, his ironic ''success'' as a physician of the gouty upper class, seem merely punitive rather than tragically inevitable.

But whether or not there is final inevitability in the collapse of Lydgate's ideal, he does illustrate the tragic paradox that the failed hero learns from the flaws that destroy him. Lydgate is improved by the correction of his assumptions about money and women. When he learns to value Dorothea, we are able to participate fully in her pity for him.

In short, the specifics of character and event induce appropriate sympathy for Lydgate. The feelings and judgments aroused concerning him and those around him are coherent with represented facts, marred but little by uncertainty or discrepancy in the interpretation. Dorothea may seem a more lovable, admirable character than Lydgate because she has a finer moral sense from the start, but in terms of the novel's subject, theme, and required rhetoric, only Lydgate is successfully established as a tragic protagonist. Ultimately, he draws more sympathy than Dorothea because his aims, though not higher than hers, are more specific, more capable of fulfillment and thus of tragic loss. Casaubon dies after only eighteen months of marriage, leaving Dorothea not a ruined life but wealth, freedom, and a chance to start over on her aims; whereas Lydgate's life and possibilities really undergo a slow deterioration. And while Dorothea is satisfied with her second marriage (whether or not the reader is meant to be), Lydgate never is resigned to his fate. Dorothea stirs pity for what *perhaps* she might have been, Lydgate for what he and we firmly believe he could have been.

It is regrettable that an analysis of *Middlemarch* must, like the novel itself, continually remind us of its one great weakness. For though our distance from Dorothea is maladjusted, and though her status as a protagonist makes this a very serious failure, the novel remains George Eliot's most unified and rhetorically successful fiction. It would be a worthwhile experiment to find a sensitive student wholly unfamiliar with *Middlemarch* and have him read it, omitting the Prelude and pausing at the death of Casaubon to evaluate Dorothea and her first marriage. It can be wagered that he would see a tragic pattern working up to that point and that, except for some ambiguity about Will, his responses would be in harmony with that pattern. Even when we look at Dorothea's story beyond that point and at the Prelude, we still must say that the novel is not irreparably damaged by them, nor is its superior position in George Eliot's canon.

For in this portrait of provincial England, George Eliot placed more characters with a far more appropriate perspective and relative prominence, a more consistent representation and interpretation than was generally true in the previous novels. After considering as fully as possible the techniques by which an artist creates distance, the severest critic must concur in Blackwood's opinion that in *Middlemarch* George Eliot repeated and even exceeded all her previous triumphs (*GEL*, 5:149).

Notes

1. George Eliot, "Notes on Form in Art," in *Essays of George Eliot*, ed. Thomas Pinney (New York: Columbia University Press, 1963), pp. 433, 434.

2. Critics discussing unity and subject matter include Walter Allen, *George Eliot* (New York: Macmillan, 1964), pp. 151, 269; Quentin Anderson, "George Eliot in *Middlemarch*," in *From Dickens to Hardy*, Pelican Guide to English Literature, vol. 6. ed. Boris Ford (Baltimore, Md.: Penguin Books, 1958), pp. 276-77; David Daiches, *George Eliot: Middlemarch* (London: Edward Arnold, 1963), p. 7; Leslie Stephen, *George Eliot* (London: Macmillan, 1926), p. 174; Jerome Thale, *The Novels of George Eliot* (New York: Columbia University Press, 1959), pp. 107-8; Frederick Willey, "Appearance and Reality in *Middlemarch*," *Southern Review* 5 (1969): 419. One of the few modern critics who diverge from this agreement is Arnold Kettle, *An Introduction to the English Novel*, 2 vols. (New York: Harper and Row, 1960), 1: 183-84.

Various aspects of the theme have been discussed by Ian Adam, "Character and Destiny in George Eliot's Fiction," *Nineteenth Century Fiction* 20 (1965): 127-43; Allen, p. 95; Calvin Bedient, *Architects of the Self: George Eliot, D. H. Lawrence, and E. M. Forster* (Berkeley: University of California Press, 1972), pp. 80-97; Bedient, "Middlemarch: Touching Down," *Hudson Review* 22 (1969): 70-84; Joan Bennett, *George Eliot: Her Mind and Her Art* (Cambridge: University Press, 1948), p. 162; Review in *Spectator*, 7 December 1872, reprinted in *George Eliot: The Critical Heritage*, ed. David

Carroll (New York: Barnes and Noble, 1971), pp. 308-9; Daiches, pp. 57-58; Reva Stump, *Movement and Vision in George Eliot's Novels* (Seattle: University of Washington Press, 1959), p. 137.

The various plots are discussed by: Walter Allen, *The English Novel* (New York: E. P. Dutton and Co., 1954), p. 269; Anderson, p. 278; Carroll, ed., pp. 306-8; Bert Hornback, "The Moral Imagination of George Eliot," *Papers on Language and Literature* 8 (1972): 384; Henry James, "Middlemarch," *Galaxy* (March 1873), reprinted in *The House of Fiction*, ed. Leon Edel (London: Rupert Hart-Davis, 1957), pp. 260-61; Mark Schorer, "The Structure of the Novel," in *Middlemarch: Critical Approaches to the Novel*, ed. Barbara Hardy (London: University of London, The Athlone Press, 1967), pp. 12-13; Newton P. Stallknecht, "Resolution and Independence: A Reading of *Middlemarch*," in *Twelve Original Essays on Great English Novels*, ed. Charles Shapiro (Detroit, Mich.: Wayne State University Press, 1960), p. 125.

See also chap. 2, n. 3, above, for my own reasons for calling this novel a qualified tragedy.

3. Sidney Colvin, review in *The Fortnightly Review*, 19 January 1873, reprinted in *George Eliot and Her Readers*, ed. Laurence Lerner and John Holstrom (New York: Barnes and Noble, 1966), p. 104.

4. Ibid., p. 105.

5. These are the three main ways, with much variant shading, in which the marriage is viewed by critics, all of whom discuss it to some extent. George Eliot would have reason to groan again over readers who wished the novel to be something quite different from what it is (*GEL*, 5:441). But she herself did not make clear what it is in this part.

6. Jerome Beaty, *Middlemarch from Notebook to Novel: A Study of George Eliot's Creative Method*, Illinois Studies in Language and Literature, vol. 47 (Urbana: University of Illinois Press, 1960), p. 9.

7. Ibid., pp. 3-4.

8. George Eliot, *Middlemarch*, Standard Edition in 3 vols. (Edinburgh: William Blackwood and Sons, 189-?), 1:142, chap. 11. As with previous novels, citations refer first to volume and page of this edition and then to the chapter number for the benefit of users of other editions.

9. Joseph Munt Langford of Blackwood's firm raised this question even before the novel's publication, *GEL*, 5:207. Daiches, pp. 9-10, and W. J. Harvey, *The Art of George Eliot* (New York: Oxford University Press, 1962), pp. 128-29, make the best defenses of the delay.

10. Beaty, pp. 52-55. The changes were made so that Dorothea's, Lydgate's, and Fred's stories would be included in each serial issue, but the rhetorical effects are more important than that.

11. Various aspects of this have been criticized by Allen, *George Eliot*, p. 159; Beaty, pp. 74-75; Bennett, p. 170; Harvey, p. 144.

12. Beaty, pp. 25–42.

13. Significant discussions of the narrator's knowledge and techniques are offered by most critics. See especially Isobel Armstrong, "*Middlemarch*: A Note on George Eliot's 'Wisdom,' " in *Critical Essays on George Eliot*, ed. Barbara Hardy (London: Routledge and Kegan Paul, 1970), pp. 116-32; Anderson, pp. 279-90; John Halperin, *The Language of Meditation: Four Studies in Nineteenth Century Fiction* (Ilfracombe, Devon: Arthur H. Stockwell, 1973), pp. 58-60; W. Erwin Hester, "George Eliot's Technique as

a Novelist'' (Ph.D. diss., University of North Carolina, 1961), chap. 1; U. C. Knoepflmacher, *George Eliot's Early Novels: The Limits of Realism* (Berkeley: University of California Press, 1968), pp. 178-88; F. R. Leavis, *The Great Tradition* (New York: New York University Press, 1963), pp. 61-79; J. Hillis Miller, *The Form of Victorian Fiction* (Notre Dame, Ind.: University of Notre Dame Press, 1968), pp. 84-85, 113; K. M. Newton, ''The Role of the Narrator in George Eliot's Novels,'' *Journal of Narrative Technique* 3 (1973): 97-107.

14. Colvin, p. 103.

15. The reader's response to Dorothea in relation to Casaubon is discussed by Daiches, pp. 19-20, and by Laurence Lerner, *The Truthtellers: Jane Austen, George Eliot, D. H. Lawrence* (New York: Schocken Books, 1967), pp. 260-64.

16. Sumner Ferris has called it heartless, ''*Middlemarch*, George Eliot's Masterpiece,'' in *From Jane Austen to Joseph Conrad*, ed. Robert C. Rathburn and Martin Steinmann (Minneapolis: University of Minnesota Press, 1958), pp. 203-4. I disagree and consider it a necessary response that should have beeen made in Casaubon's life, had Dorothea been capable of it. After his death it has a quality of vengeance for his codicil, but it is still necessary and still infused with her pity for him. But the narrator's judgment is not clear.

17. The character analyses of both Will and Dorothea and the judgments on their marriage are too numerous to document here. Every critic has had his say, and it is probably impossible to say anything new or to resolve the debates. But it may be possible to point more specifically to techniques of rhetoric that create such varied analyses and evaluations of major characters.

18. Daiches, p. 44.

19. It may also betray sexual repression in her or others. Among the critics who have analyzed the portrayal of sexuality in the novel, see Laura Comer Emery, *George Eliot's Creative Conflict: The Other Side of Silence* (Berkeley: University of California Press, 1976), chap. 5; Hardy, *The Novels of George Eliot*, pp. 65, 145; Hardy, *The Appropriate Form: An Essay on the Novel* (London: University of London, Athlone Press, 1964), pp. 105-31; Harvey, pp. 196-97.

20. Beaty, pp. 40-41.

Daniel Deronda: Conclusion

Middlemarch is almost universally acknowledged as the pinnacle of George Eliot's achievement. But she did not stop there, and her final novel, *Daniel Deronda*, must be considered in some measure, especially in any study of her rhetoric. For the virtues and defects of *Daniel Deronda* are largely matters of rhetoric, of techniques that have caused the intense admiration or alienation of readers from the first publication.[1]

Yet one comes to the rhetorical analysis of *Daniel Deronda* with a strong sense of *déja vu*. Many of its features have appeared in the previous novels and have been analyzed in the previous chapters of this book. Like *Adam Bede* and *Felix Holt*, this novel has a sermonizing male hero whose deficiencies are not adequately interpreted, together with a religious enthusiast dehumanized by perfect virtue and incredible speech patterns (Mordecai is far, far more distanced this way than Mr. Lyon or even Dinah Morris[2]). Like *The Mill on the Floss* and *Middlemarch*, it has a protagonist yearning to know where in the wide world one can best employ great sympathies and intelligence. For Deronda's yearning and character, the narrator shows a sympathy even less critical than for Maggie's and Dorothea's. Like *Felix Holt*, *Deronda* has a political issue not made sufficiently interesting and important in itself and not well integrated into a central theme; it also has two plots poorly balanced and connected, one of which critics have always wanted to throw away.[3] But like all the previous novels, *Deronda* represents a feminine egoist moving out of herself, and Gwendolen is, of all of them, the most fully represented and accurately, relentlessly interpreted.

The rhetoric of *Daniel Deronda*, then, has not so many specific differences from the other novels; rather, it intensifies both the worst and best of George Eliot's techniques. It may serve, therefore, as a summary illustration of them.

Of all Eliot's novels, *Deronda* alone is not a coherent whole. No one statement of what-it's-about will define its subject. The best suggestions fail to persuade. The novel cannot be all about the education of Deronda, effected by his contacts with Gwendolen and Mordecai,[4] because Gwendolen has obviously too much independent value, is too clearly the center of her own story. Nor is the whole satisfactorily defined as the story of two characters rising out of personal deficiencies, Gwendolen out of egoism and Deronda out of aimless neutrality.[5] Deronda is never felt as inherently deficient; his lack of direction, though noted, seems always due to his circumstances, not to his character. Further, though Deronda acts to change Gwendolen's deficiencies and course of life, she has no such function in his life. Their stories are not two interlocking versions of the same subject, as were Dorothea's and Lydgate's.

We might say that the subject is the search for a role in life, to be found by Gwendolen on the personal level and by Deronda on the social. In that case, the unifying theme would be similar to *Middlemarch*'s, a statement of the necessity of altruism in any worthy role. But that definition confronts us with another rhetorical problem, the lack of satisfactory resolution of either search. Despite all the historic seriousness of Zionism, Deronda's sailing away to the East with his perfect wife seems a voyage into never-never land, not into a valid social function. As for Gwendolen, she will be a good woman, but what else will she be? The Widow of Offendene, kind to her aging mother and sustained in virtue by letters from the East? Or the wife of Rex Gascoigne? Both resolutions are suggested. If the virtuous widowhood is seriously contemplated, it becomes as sentimental—or comic—as Deronda's denouement. If the marriage is not to occur, then the revival of Rex's feeling in Chapter 58 has no purpose. And neither resolution is fully acceptable as a sphere in which "one of the best of women" will be able to "make others glad that they were born."[6] If we have here a deliberate irresolution of plot, it is not clearly purposeful. Why should Gwendolen's life-role be left more uncertain than Deronda's? And how shall we respond to her indefinite and possibly dismal fate?

Even if the novel had a clearly delineated subject and resolution of it, coherence would be damaged by the lack of structural alternations and connections such as held *Middlemarch* together so well. Of the first thirty-one chapters, twenty-four deal exclusively with Gwendolen's story; Deronda encounters her in two others but speaks to her only in one, and his story is allotted only the five-chapter flashback on his early life. Then, after she is married, she gets only five chapters exclusively, and never more than one at a time. She and Deronda engage in dialogue at varying lengths in nine chapters. The other twenty-six chapters are all his story, in which she has no part at all. Thus the first near-half of the novel is almost all about Gwendolen, the second half-plus almost all about Deronda. And in that second half, Gwendolen appears chiefly as his "penitent." No wonder, then, that a reader feels he is reading first one novel, then another, and is hard put to see any thematic connection between them.

The lack of structural alternation also accentuates the differences in characterization and style between the two stories,[7] making more obvious the fascination of Gwendolen's and the alienating dullness of Deronda's. The second half causes chiefly an irritable wish to get away from Mordecai's talk and Deronda's doubts and to return to Gwendolen and the effects of her marital choice.

But clearly, the failure of structural rhetoric would not have been so damaging could we have given equal credence, sympathy, and interest to the second story. But not even the most vigorous contemporary defenders of the novel pretend that the Deronda story wins those responses. Without repetition of all the common criticisms of this part of the novel, several specific rhetorical problems may be pointed out.

The representation of Deronda is a failure, first because he is not dramatized in ordinary events. A kind of excuse is offered in the explanations that ''what he was'' was not all ''evident in ordinary intercourse'' (2:131, chap. 32) and that his wide sympathies prevented his acting in a partisan cause. But presumably he does act in daily relationships; yet we see almost nothing that would indicate his character and narrow his distance from the reader. Instead of such credible dramatized events, we have the chain of improbable and melodramatic ones—chance encounters, psychic intuitions and responses, revelations before impending deaths, and the like.[8] And even in those scenes, Deronda mostly listens and thinks; he says and does little unless moved to a stagy passion.

These improbable events ruin the representation of Deronda as a natural person. Only a ''rescuing angel,'' not a man, could not merely disconcert a pretty gambler with his staring but also cause her to start losing. What ordinary man would have chanced to see Gwendolen going into the shop at early morning, have known her business inside, and have undone it within the hour? This aura of the supernatural intensifies at the recognition scene at Blackfriars Bridge; Deronda's nature is ''too large'' not to be ''wrought upon'' by the prophetic call of his destiny. And with equal clairvoyance he can leap to the certainty of Mordecai's relation to Mirah without asking his family name or his reason for not using his first name. The reason for all these improbabilities, of course, is the schema of the plot, and the logic of human character must yield to that.

Even when Deronda is not represented supernaturally, he remains less than humanly interesting and sympathetic. His typical posture, standing and grasping his coat collar, makes him a kind of Napoleonic statue; his passionate dropping at the knees of his mother or Gwendolen makes him the hero of a cheap melodrama. His dialogue is mostly stilted and unnatural, even with Sir Hugo, and always with Mirah and Mordecai; in his counseling sessions with Gwendolen, he delivers lecturettes. (Perhaps our one moment of sympathy with Grandcourt occurs at his request to "excuse me the sermon" [2:91, chap. 29].)

Nor are the other characters in this plot represented more successfully. Neither Mirah nor Mordecai is credible in their morally perfect and almost inanimate characters or in their romantic histories, recited in elegant poetic prose; the closer they get to Deronda, the more he recedes in the mist. Hans Meyrick is credible as a dilettante artist but less so as rival lover of Mirah (it is the failure of Ladislaw again). Only the Cohens and Sir Hugo talk and act naturally, and briefly cause Deronda to do so.

An attempt is made to compensate for this lack of dramatic representation by lengthy narrative analysis of the characters' thoughts and moral proclivities. This method is not inherently defective; it served superbly to reveal Lydgate, Rosamond, and Bulstrode. But in the case of Deronda and his friends, the analysis is less a revelation of character than a set of directives to the reader made by emotive diction: "reverence, tenderness, fervour, awe, anguish, compassion, pity," and—over and over—"solemnity." Naming the emotion of the character dictates that it shall occur in the reader, regardless of what is or is not otherwise represented. Deronda's "anguish" finally *is* "intolerable"—and not just to himself.

The alienating representations in this plot are aggravated by blindly admiring interpretations, especially of Deronda. No one is subjected to even so much criticism as was leveled at Dorothea's and Ladislaw's posturings, let alone to the cool-headed evaluation given Lydgate. Neither the characters nor the narrator properly perform this function for the implied author.

The characters' judgments cannot be trusted. The mutual admiration society of Deronda-Mirah-Mordecai-the Meyricks is patently intended to engage the reader, despite the sentimental goodness, despite Mordecai's insensibility to concerns outside his vision, despite his condescending view of the "ignorance" and "spiritual poverty" of the Cohens who shelter him (3:40, chap. 46). Mordecai's Zionist hope, his expectation of an alter ego, and his instant interpretation of Daniel as his fulfillment are clearly meant to convince the reader as they do Daniel. But since the facts suggest fanaticism and manipulation as much as prophetic vision and influence, the reader cannot accept the view either has of the other. Of all the characters, only Hans ever needles Deronda; and when he does so, in the "Stage direction" of his letter (3:153-54, chap. 52), the narrator has already presented Deronda in that attitude too often and too seriously for us to suppose that we ought to identify with Hans's mockery in any but his affectionate mood.

The narrator, no more than the characters, seems able to interpret according to facts. We are told explicitly that Mordecai's yearning embodies the "mature spiritual need" of a "fuller nature," of "an ideal life straining to embody itself"; it is to be spoken of with reverence (2:300-301, chap. 38), not with incredulity or even pity. Deronda is interpreted most often by a silence that gives consent to his own evaluations of people and events, with no intimations of his errors or character defects. His instant and fervid admiration for his grandfather shows no sense of the man's impersonal tyranny over Deronda's mother (of which she *has* convinced the reader). And his parting comfort to Gwendolen (that they would have felt their differences more—meaning, apparently, his superiority—but now may have nearer minds) is, indeed, even harder than it "seemed" to himself. But in both cases, what Deronda's thoughts and words suggest as marks of insensitivity, the narrator seems to accept as just the opposite.[9]

The surest signal of the narrator's uncritical identification with Deronda is the exact similarity of their styles. It would be risky to wager on the source of the following passage:

> Suppose the stolen offspring of some mountain tribe brought up in a city of the plain, or one with an inherited genius for painting, and born blind—the ancestral life would lie within them as a dim longing for unknown objects and sensations, and the spell-bound habit of their inherited frames would be like a cunningly-wrought musical instrument, never played on, but quivering throughout in uneasy mysterious moanings of its in-

tricate structure that, under the right touch, gives music.
(3:315, chap. 63)

The involved, heavy syntax, compounded analogies, and laudatory diction are just what the narrator too often produces in this part of the novel; but the passage is in a speech of Deronda to Mordecai. Examples could be multiplied in which the same turgid prose represents what Deronda ''said to himself'' and what the narrator says about him. In this case, such diction as ''genius,'' ''dim longing,'' ''cunningly wrought'' and ''intricate structure'' implies Deronda's superior nature; while ''stolen,'' ''born blind'' and ''spell-bound'' supposedly explain and justify both his previous inertia and his sudden power to reverse the orientation of his whole previous education and experience. The ''right touch'' and ''music'' tell us to approve fully both Mordecai's psychic pressure on Deronda and the result of it in his new goal, which he now calls an ''ideal task.'' The narrator affirms this judgment by saying that his ''decided pledge of himself'' had ''sacramental solemnity'' for both men. In both representation and interpretation, character and narrator have merged. But the reader is left far away in the world of reality.

The reader who cannot believe in Deronda's mission to restore Zion has also a difficulty with his mission to save Gwendolen Harleth. It is not the fact of his role that strains credulity, but the way it is worked out in their encounters. His supernaturalism, more than her own personality, accounts for her instantly and totally adopting him as her conscience. His posturing infects her in their longer joint scenes, especially the ''confession'' scene in Genoa where most of their gestures and speeches make a soap opera out of a genuinely intense situation. Indeed, the worst effect of the rhetorical failure with Deronda is the harm he does to Gwendolen's characterization.

For, apart from her response to Deronda, Gwendolen is George Eliot's rhetorical masterpiece. Because she is a more complete egoist than Esther Lyon and Mrs. Transome and can change more than Hetty Sorrel or Rosamond Vincy, she is more a

challenge than any of them. The egoism must be revealed so that
the reader will comprehend her and maintain sympathy; the
change must be credibly accounted for. With her, George Eliot
succeeds by techniques antithetical to those used on Deronda.

Whereas Deronda's story lacked credible actions, in Gwendolen's they abound. Social gatherings and contests of the rural
gentry, charades and horseback riding, gambling in a spa,
bankruptcy and its consequences, family discussions and quarrels—all these events provide natural settings for the dramatic
representation of Gwendolen's worst and best qualities. They
credibly reveal her mental biases and suggest those characteristics
on which Deronda can work. The moments of "repentance"
toward her mother, sister, and Rex prepare us to believe that
remorse and self-knowledge can enter her marital relationship and
even change her character when the occasion for them becomes
severe enough. It is not surprising that she reacts to a mentor, only that she does it so swiftly and intensely before the occasion
becomes severe.

Unlike Deronda, Gwendolen is fully realized in conversations
with other lively and credible speakers. Of the first fifteen
chapters, ten contain such dialogues, and in the others she is
either alone or absent or well represented by the narrator. These
dialogues make her egoism evident but understandable by the
contrast with others. She is antipathetic, but hope for her is encouraged.

Because Gwendolen's reactions and character change are the
issue in her story, the narrative representation and analysis of her
mind are required and are provided in appropriate quantity and
clear prose. A typical passage reveals her own and others'
characters, foreshadows consequences, and implies a valid interpretation:

> She was very well satisfied with Grandcourt. His answers to
> her lively questions . . . bore drawling very well. . . . she had
> noticed that he knew what to say; and she was constantly feel-
> ing not only that he had nothing of the fool in his composition,
> but that . . . he communicated to her the impression that all

the folly lay with other people, who did what he did not care to do. A man who seems to have been able to command the best, has a sovereign power of depreciation. Then Grandcourt's behaviour as a lover had hardly at all passed the limit of an amorous homage which . . . spent all its effect in a gratified vanity. (2:74, chap. 29)

The ironic distance between her satisfaction and the narrator's knowledge is everywhere apparent. All the folly lies in Gwendolen's interpretation of her fiancé, and in her assumptions that he and she will care to do the same things, that she is the best and will never be depreciated, that his homage will last and his coldness continue to be gratifying. The last two words are an explicit judgment, substantiated by all the actions and dialogues that preceded it. Here, although the character's thought is described, the narrator merges, not with the character and her erroneous views, but really with the reader, in a shared knowledge that must be both critical and sympathetic.

Given the wrong Gwendolen does in marrying Grandcourt, we must have special reason to pity her when she reaps her harvest of misery. This reason is given in the presentation of Grandcourt. Our first views of him are external, what Gwendolen sees and hears, so that we understand her deception about him even while her own thoughts create a warning of it. Later expositions of his mind are brief but effective in revealing his absolute disrespect for others and absolute desire for mastery—all we need to know to understand his courtship and marriage.

We may, however, need to see more of him in the marriage. Grandcourt as a husband lives during only six chapters and exchanges words with Gwendolen only about a dozen times. Most of these dialogues are extremely brief; only Chapters 35, 48, and 54 contain substantial scenes. And they are widely spaced between great chunks of Deronda's story in its most melodramatic phases. Consequently, we do not know quite enough of Gwendolen's daily married life—how much of it she must spend in her husband's company, how much he restricts her normal activities. And we do not feel the continual pressure on her (as we did feel that on Lydgate), which we should feel in order to sympathize with her helplessness, hatred, and hesitation to save Grandcourt.

Though these postmarital dialogues are insufficient in quantity, they are perfect in kind and registered again in Gwendolen's afterthoughts. These thoughts now represent her husband accurately enough for the narrator and reader to join in her assessment. Grandcourt is the only major character whom George Eliot made totally unsympathetic, but he is never treated unfairly. And he has precisely the right kind (if not intensity) of effect on our distance from Gwendolen. He, not Deronda, wins our sympathy for her. As the rhetoric of character interaction failed in the cases of Deronda-Mirah and Deronda-Mordecai, in like proportion it succeeds in the case of Gwendolen-Grandcourt.

The deformity of *Daniel Deronda*, then, is largely owing to the attempted fusion of a rhetorical failure with a rhetorical success. The critic is boggled by such a phenomenon and deeply puzzled that George Eliot, the author of *Middlemarch*, could not see what she had done.[10] Fortunately, the present study is an attempt to analyze the novels, not their author, so that one can rest with the statement that if Daniel and his friends are a sad ending to George Eliot's fictions, Gwendolen and her society remain to represent her best powers and keep her last novel alive in the interest and appreciation of her readers.

In the end, one has the feeling that *Daniel Deronda* should have been composed before *Middlemarch*, and that if Gwendolen had come first, Dorothea might have been better. *Middlemarch* has *Deronda*'s weaknesses only in Dorothea's relation to Will, but has its strengths well developed everywhere else. *Middlemarch*, therefore, is the climax of George Eliot's artistic development, and it will serve for a summary of her progress in the three categories of fictional rhetoric: plot, character, and narration.

With *Middlemarch* George Eliot achieves both unity and meaningful complexity in plot; these rise from a definite subject, credible parallels and interrelations of people, and from their internal reactions more than from tangled external events. In all parts of the plot, dramatic scenes are adequately provided and balanced with narration. Despite the number of events and scenes, few are overdone; each is developed and placed to make its contribution to the effect of the whole. The moral issues in the plot are George Eliot's most subtle; there are no obvious external criteria by which Dorothea and Lydgate should decide their marriages or most other questions affecting the welfare of their fellows. Consequently, their struggles, decisions, and resulting actions have a keener interest and pathos than were achieved in the early novels.

The issues of plot are embodied in characters, whose development and interaction are the chief source of interest and sympathy in any George Eliot novel. Her most important advance, therefore, was in creating psychologically complex people and distancing them by their relations to each other. The principals of *Middlemarch* are not static; they call for constant reconsideration of their motives and are capable of surprising us. Minor and choral characters do not obscure the conflicts of the principals; Mrs. Dollop's patrons, for instance, create real problems and real pity for Lydgate. The novel's one major flaw in character rhetoric is obvious—Ladislaw's confused and unappealing portrayal, which confuses the representation and interpretation of Dorothea. But aside from that, one can hardly cite an instance in which the characters, major and minor, moral or immoral, shrewd or stupid, do not successfully guide our judgments and sympathy by their opinions of each other, their statements, and their behavior.

George Eliot's Victorian style made her ultimate success as a rhetorician depend on her ability to refine her narrator. By the writing of *Middlemarch*, the early "real" and almost shrewish narrator has developed into the knowledgeable and sympathetic person whom the reader instinctively trusts. Her relation to the characters is steady and clearsighted, almost free of pugnacious attacks or defenses or uncritical admiration. *Middlemarch* shows a lingering instability in the narrator's judgment of Ladislaw and of

Dorothea in relation to him, but also a greatly increased firmness of judgment in all other cases, together with flexibility in taking account of all the factors involved. Rosamond, Casaubon, and Bulstrode are antipathetic characters, but critics do not say George Eliot disliked them or treated them unfairly. In relation to the reader, the narrator displays a genuine unity of feeling based on an assumption of the reader's intelligence and right feeling. This rapport allows for the further union of both narrator and reader with the experience and feeling of all mankind.

In refining her judgments, George Eliot's narrator has also learned to fuse them naturally with description and analysis. *Middlemarch* contains no "pauses" and few isolated pronouncements. The moral traits of Dorothea, Casaubon, Rosamond, and many others are implied by description of their appearances, gestures, characteristic speech, and thought processes. Those who speak, act, or think but little are analyzed with diction that subtly guides evaluation. Such a method keeps the reader in the story, mentally involved with the characters and thus with the intellectual and emotional responses suggested.

George Eliot's stated aim as artist was the extension of her readers' understanding and sympathy even to characters who might differ from themselves in all but basic humanity. Such an aim demanded all the skills of rhetoric. By developing them throughout her career, she accomplished her aim, as far as we can judge from the novels themselves and the comments of readers. Certainly her efforts made her a technically better novelist. One may therefore reassert that her progress as literary artist may be fruitfully studied and accurately assessed in terms of her rhetoric.

Notes

1. A still excelling summary of these opinions is Henry James, "*Daniel Deronda*: A Conversation," *The Atlantic Monthly* 38 (1876), reprinted in *George Eliot: A Collection of Critical Essays*, ed. George R. Creeger (Englewood Cliffs, N.J.: Prentice-Hall, Inc., 1970), pp. 161-76.

2. See Joan Bennett, *George Eliot: Her Mind and Her Art* (Cambridge: University Press, 1948), pp. 185-89, and W. J. Harvey, *The Art of George Eliot* (New York: Oxford University Press, 1962), pp. 184-85, for analyses of George Eliot's failure with Mordecai.

3. F. R. Leavis, *The Great Tradition* (New York: New York University Press, 1963), p. 122, contains the serious and famous suggestion of such a division, first made in *Scrutiny* in 1946. Leavis rescinds that suggestion in his introduction to the novel (New York: Harper Torchbooks, 1961), p. xiv.

4. David R. Carroll, ''The Unity of *Daniel Deronda*.'' *Essays in Criticism* 9 (1959): 369-80.

5. Edward Dowden in *Contemporary Review* (February 1877), reprinted in *George Eliot: The Critical Heritage*, ed. David R. Carroll (New York: Barnes and Noble, 1971), pp. 439-40.

6. George Eliot, *Daniel Deronda*, Standard Edition in 3 vols. (Edinburgh: William Blackwood and Sons, 189-?), 3:407, chap. 70. As with previous novels, citations refer first to volume and page of this edition and then to chapter number for the benefit of users of other editions.

7. Jerome Beaty, ''*Daniel Deronda* and the Question of Unity in Fiction,'' *Victorian Newsletter* 15 (1959): 16-20, discusses these differences and their prevention of a unified effect in this novel.

8. Bennett, p. 186, lists the improbabilities in detail.

9. Carole Robinson, ''The Severe Angel: A Study of *Daniel Deronda*,'' *ELH* 31 (1964): 282-83, discusses George Eliot's failure to validate Deronda's supposed tender feeling in face of the evidences of his anger and coldness.

10. That she did not see is clear from her letters, especially the much-quoted expression of displeasure with critics who failed to see the relationships she intended, *GEL*, 6:290.

Bibliography

Primary Sources

NOTE: There is no modern definitive edition of George Eliot's novels, though Gordon Haight has this important work in progress (1980). The nearest-to-definitive editions are the Cabinet, the Standard, and the Warwick editions from George Eliot's first publishers, Blackwood's in Edinburgh; at least one of these is usually found in college and university libraries. Today the best, most accessible editions are the paperbound reprints edited by contemporary scholars, yet these go into new editions or out of print with disconcerting frequency. In the hope of making my references to the Eliot novels most useful to students and teachers of Eliot, I have used the Standard Edition from Blackwood's, giving volume and page numbers, and also giving chapter numbers for the benefit of users of other editions.

Cross, John Walter, ed. *George Eliot's Life as Related in Her Letters and Journals*. 3 vols. Boston: Houghton Mifflin Co., 1909.

Eliot, George. *The Works of George Eliot*. Standard Edition. 21 vols. Edinburgh: William Blackwood and Sons, 189-?.

Haight, Gordon S., ed. *The George Eliot Letters*. 7 vols. New Haven, Conn.: Yale University Press, 1954-55.

Pinney, Thomas, ed. *Essays of George Eliot*. New York: Columbia University Press, 1963.

Secondary Sources

Adam, Ian. "Character and Destiny in George Eliot's Fiction." *Nineteenth Century Fiction* 20 (1965): 127–43.

Allen, Walter. *The English Novel*. New York: E. P. Dutton and Co., 1954.

———. *George Eliot*. New York: Macmillan, 1964.

Anderson, Quentin. "George Eliot in *Middlemarch*." In *From Dickens to Hardy*. Pelican Guide to English Literature, vol. 6, edited by Boris Ford. Baltimore, Md.: Penguin Books, 1958.

Beaty, Jerome. "*Daniel Deronda* and the Question of Unity in Fiction." *Victorian Newsletter* 15 (1959): 16–20.

———. *Middlemarch from Notebook to Novel: A Study of George Eliot's Creative Method*. Illinois Studies in Language and Literature, vol. 47. Urbana: University of Illinois Press, 1960.

Bedient, Calvin. *Architects of the Self: George Eliot, D. H. Lawrence and E. M. Forster*. Berkeley: University of California Press, 1972.

———. "Middlemarch: Touching Down." *Hudson Review* 22 (1969): 70–84.

Bennett, Joan. *George Eliot: Her Mind and Her Art*. Cambridge: University Press, 1948.

Bonaparte, Felicia. *Will and Destiny: Morality and Tragedy in George Eliot's Novels*. New York: New York University Press, 1975.

Booth, Wayne. *The Rhetoric of Fiction*. Chicago: University of Chicago Press, 1961.

———. "*The Rhetoric of Fiction* and the Poetics of Fictions." *Novel: A Forum on Fiction* 1 (1968): 105–17.

Bradbury, Malcolm. "Towards a Poetics of Fiction: An Approach through Structure." *Novel: A Forum on Fiction* 1 (1967): 45–52.

Brown, E. K. *Rhythm in the Novel*. Toronto: University of Toronto Press, 1950.

Brown, Keith. "The Ending of *The Mill on the Floss*." *Notes and Queries* 11 (1964): 226.

Buckler, Wm. E. "Memory, Morality and the Tragic Vision in the Early Novels of George Eliot." In *The English Novel in the Nineteenth Century: Essays on the Literary Mediation of Human Values*, edited by George Goodin. Urbana: University of Illinois Press, 1972.

Bullett, Gerald. *George Eliot: Her Life and Books*. London: Collins Press, 1947.

Bullough, Edward, " 'Psychical Distance' as a Factor in Art and an Aesthetic Principle." In *The Problems of Aesthetics*, edited by Eliseo Vivas and Murray Krieger. New York: Holt, Rinehart and Winston, 1953.

Carroll, David R. "*Felix Holt*: Society as Protagonist." *Nineteenth Century Fiction* 17 (1962): 237–52.

———, ed. *George Eliot: The Critical Heritage*. New York: Barnes & Noble, 1971.

———. "The Unity of *Daniel Deronda*." *Essays in Criticism* 9 (1959): 369-80.

Crane, R. S. "The Concept of Plot and the Plot of 'Tom Jones.' " In *Critics and Criticism*, edited by R. S. Crane. Chicago: University of Chicago Press, Phoenix Books, 1957.

———. *The Language of Criticism and the Structure of Poetry*. Toronto: University of Toronto Press, 1953.

Creeger, George R., ed. *George Eliot: A Collection of Critical Essays*. Englewood Cliffs, N.J.: Prentice-Hall, Inc., 1970.

———. "An Interpretation of *Adam Bede*." ELH 23 (1956): 218–38.

Daiches, David. *George Eliot: Middlemarch*. London: Edward Arnold, 1963.

———. *A Study of Literature for Readers and Critics*. Ithaca, N.Y.: Cornell University Press, 1948.

Diekhoff, John S. "The Happy Ending of *Adam Bede*." *ELH* 3 (1936): 221–27.

Drew, Elizabeth. *The Novel: A Modern Guide to Fifteen English Masterpieces*. New York: Dell Publishing Co., 1963.

Eastman, Richard. *A Guide to the Novel*. San Francisco, Cal.: Chandler Publications, 1965.

Emery, Laura Comer. *George Eliot's Creative Conflict: The Other Side of Silence*. Berkeley: University of California Press, 1976.

Friedman, Norman. *Form and Meaning in Fiction*. Athens: University of Georgia Press, 1975.

Frye, Northrop. *Anatomy of Criticism: Four Essays*. Princeton, N.J.: Princeton University Press, 1957.

Garrett, Peter K. *Scene and Symbol from George Eliot to James Joyce: Studies in Changing Fictional Mode*. New Haven, Conn.: Yale University Press, 1969.

Gibson, Walker. "Authors, Speakers, Readers and Mock Readers." *College English* 11 (1950): 265–69.

Goodman, Paul. *The Structure of Literature*. Chicago: University of Chicago Press, 1954.

Hagan, John. "A Reinterpretation of *The Mill on the Floss*." *PMLA* 87 (1972): 53–68.

Haight, Gordon S., ed. *A Century of George Eliot Criticism*. Boston: Houghton Mifflin Co., 1965.

Halperin, John. *The Language of Meditation: Four Studies in Nineteenth Century Fiction*. Elms Court, Ifracombe, Devon: Arthur H. Stockwell, Ltd., 1973.

Hardy, Barbara. *The Appropriate Form: An Essay on the Novel*. London: University of London, Athlone Press, 1964.

———, ed. *Critical Essays on George Eliot*. London: Routledge and Kegan Paul, 1970.

———, ed. *Middlemarch: Critical Approaches to the Novel*. London: University of London, The Athlone Press, 1967.

———. *The Novels of George Eliot*. London: University of London, The Athlone Press, 1959.

———. "Towards a Poetics of Fiction: 3) An Approach through Narrative." *Novel: A Forum on Fiction* 2 (1968): 5–14.

Harvey, W. J. *The Art of George Eliot*. New York: Oxford University Press, 1962.

———. *Character and the Novel*. Ithaca, N.Y.: Cornell University Press, 1965.

Hester, W. Erwin. "George Eliot's Technique as a Novelist." Ph.D. dissertation, University of North Carolina, 1961.

Holstrom, John, and Lerner, Laurence, eds. *George Eliot and Her Readers*. New York: Barnes and Noble, Inc., 1966.

Hornback, Bert. "The Moral Imagination of George Eliot." *Papers on Language and Literature* 8 (1972): 380–94.

Iser, Wolfgang. *The Implied Reader: Patterns of Communication in Prose Fiction from Bunyan to Beckett*. Baltimore, Md.: The Johns Hopkins University Press, 1974.

James, Henry. "Middlemarch." *Galaxy* (March 1873). Reprinted in *The House of Fiction*, edited by Leon Edel. London: Rupert Hart-Davis, 1957, pp. 259–67.

Kettle, Arnold. *An Introduction to the English Novel*. 2 vols. New York: Harper and Row, 1960.

King, Jeanette. *Tragedy in the Victorian Novel: Theory and Practice in the Novels of George Eliot, Thomas Hardy and Henry James*. Cambridge: Cambridge University Press, 1978.

Knoepflmacher, U. C. *George Eliot's Early Novels: The Limits of Realism*. Berkeley: University of California Press, 1968.

Leavis, F. R. *The Great Tradition*. New York: New York University Press, 1963.

Lerner, Laurence. *The Truthtellers: Jane Austen, George Eliot, D. H. Lawrence*. New York: Schocken Books, 1967.

Levine, George. "Intelligence as Deception: *The Mill on the Floss*." *PMLA* 80 (1965): 402–9.

Lodge, David. *Language of Fiction: Essays in Criticism and Verbal Analysis of the English Novel*. London: Routledge and Kegan Paul, 1966.

———. "Toward a Poetics of Fiction: 2) An Approach through Language." *Novel: A Forum on Fiction* 1 (1968): 158–69.

Luecke, Sister Jane Marie. "Ladislaw and the *Middlemarch* Vision." *Nineteenth Century Fiction* 21 (1966): 35–47.

Miller, J. Hillis. *The Form of Victorian Fiction*. Notre Dame, Ind.: University of Notre Dame Press, 1968.

Newton, K. M. "The Role of the Narrator in George Eliot's Novels." *Journal of Narrative Technique* 3 (1973): 97–107.

Ong, Walter J. "The Writer's Audience Is Always a Fiction." *PMLA* 90 (1975): 9–22.

Paris, Bernard. *Experiments in Life: George Eliot's Quest for Values.* Detroit, Mich.: Wayne State University Press, 1965.

———. "Form, Theme, and Imitation in Realistic Fiction." *Novel: A Forum on Fiction* 1 (1968): 140–49.

———. *A Psychological Approach to Fiction.* Bloomington: Indiana University Press, 1974.

Rathburn, Robert C., and Steinmann, Martin, eds. *From Jane Austen to Joseph Conrad.* Minneapolis: University of Minnesota Press, 1958.

Reigelman, Milton. "Narrative Technique in George Eliot's *The Mill on the Floss*." *Kentucky Philological Association Bulletin* 3 (1976): 7–13.

Roberts, Neil. *George Eliot: Her Beliefs and Her Art.* Pittsburgh, Pa.: University of Pittsburgh Press, 1975.

Robinson, Carole. "The Severe Angel: A Study of *Daniel Deronda*." *ELH* 31 (1964): 278–300.

Sacks, Sheldon. *Fiction and the Shape of Belief.* Berkeley: University of California Press, 1964.

Scholes, Robert, and Kellogg, Robert. *The Nature of Narrative.* London: Oxford University Press, 1966.

Schorer, Mark. *The World We Imagine.* New York: Farrar, Straus and Giroux, 1968.

Shapiro, Charles, ed. *Twelve Original Essays on Great English Novels.* Detroit, Mich.: Wayne State University Press, 1960.

Slatoff, Walter J. *With Respect to Readers.* Ithaca, N.Y.: Cornell University Press, 1970.

Springer, Mary D. *Forms of the Modern Novella.* Chicago: University of Chicago Press, 1975.

Stephen, Leslie. *George Eliot.* London: Macmillan and Co., 1926.

Stevick, Philip, ed. *The Theory of the Novel.* New York: The Free Press, 1967.

Stump, Reva. *Movement and Vision in George Eliot's Novels.* Seattle: University of Washington Press, 1959.

Thale, Jerome. *The Novels of George Eliot.* New York: Columbia University Press, 1959.

Thomson, Fred. C. "The Genesis of *Felix Holt*." *PMLA* 74 (1959): 576–84.

Tillotson, Kathleen. *The Tale and the Teller.* London: Rupert Hart-Davis, 1959.

Van Ghent, Dorothy. *The English Novel: Form and Function*. New York: Harper and Row, Torchbooks, 1961.

Wellek, René, and Warren, Austin. *Theory of Literature*. New York: Harcourt, Brace and Company, 1942.

Willey, Frederick. "Appearance and Reality in *Middlemarch*." *Southern Review* 5 (1969): 419–35.

Index

NOTE: Because fictional rhetoric deals chiefly with character, the GE characters are indexed under the entry for their novels. Those barely mentioned are omitted; those mentioned on nearly every page of the chapters on their respective novels are marked with an asterisk, and only the main discussions of them in those chapters are indexed.